Sheltered by Jesus is a fascinating and deeply moving chronicle of how Jesus, using one homeless man, came knocking at the door of the unlikeliest of churches and called the pastor to provide a place for those in need to call home. What follows the pastor's response is a series of miraculous events—wrapped in everyday circumstances—that present to an unsuspecting congregation the opportunity to discover what it means to truly draw into an intensely personal relationship with our very real, living, and fatherly Creator.

— Peter J. & Roseanne M. Bolduc

Richard Berry claims to be a "dumb hick from Maine", but I would say otherwise. The Scriptures tells us that true wisdom is the fear of the Lord, and dripping from the pages of this book is the testimony of a man who has staked his life on the promise that God is a rewarder of those who earnestly seek Him. Richard's story will make you laugh with wonder at what God is able to accomplish, and will give you a window into God's heart for the things despised and deemed foolish by the world, but cherished and prized by God. God used Richard's example to nudge me further out on the limb of faith. Read this book and look for God to do the same with you.

— Sam Huggard

Co-Author of *The Five Stones An Everyday Guide To Following Jesus*, and pastor of BeFree Community Church in Alton

Sheltered by Jesus emerged from a unique vision given to Pastor Berry and the compassion that fills his heart to care enough to be the hands and feet of Jesus. As you read the stories here, you'll laugh, cry, and hopefully you'll even sense a desire to be part of something that changes others' lives. We are all homeless before Jesus rescues us, and what sets this shelter apart is Pastor Berry's desire to help the homeless find "spiritual shelter" through Jesus while providing for physical needs. Pastor Berry and the shelter embody the greatest commandments, to love God and neighbor, and my prayer is that this book will so deeply penetrate your heart that you will be compelled to love as Jesus loves.

— *Ronda Gaudette*

Vice President, Business Owner and Entrepreneur

This book will inspire us to take the focus off of ourselves and to put it onto "one of the least of these Brethren," as Jesus taught us in Matthew 25:40.

— *John Higgins*

Unity/Thorndike, Maine Amish Community

While many of us seek excellence in preaching, in facilities and organization, "the less than" often (not always) get only the leftovers. The world is rarely impressed by our excellence. But they have noticed that Richard is an instrument of God. Richard's godly dirty dozen will probably not pastor in most of our churches. But these disciples will turn the world of "the less than" right side up. Pray to God for their success because, one day, we may be in need of them. And thankful we will be that Richard started his strange journey by granting his homeless friend's odd request to sleep on a church pew on a cold winter night. And thankful we will be that he did not deviate from the call of God when 70% of his congregation left him. Richard, save a bed for me hermano!

—*Alejandro Mandes*

Director of Immigrant Mission of the Evangelical Free Church

This book contains a miraculous message of selfless love and service that will powerfully inspire and challenge you on a very deep level. Pastor Berry is a very humble man, and I know that all of the credit goes to Jesus, but he said yes every step of the way. He never gave up and never lost sight of the mission to love and serve Jesus by following his greatest command. I have no doubt that Jesus is using this small church in a small town in Maine to tell the world that He is with us and that He will use us to do wonderful things if we will just let Him!

—*Jason Dyer*
Memphis, TN

As the District Superintendent of the New England District of the Evangelical Free Church I have had the privilege of having Richard and Selma Berry as covenant friends for over 16 years. Many of us in ministry believe that the Gospel of the Kingdom transforms lives, families, and communities as Jesus impacts, changes, and reigns in more and more lives. Few of us through our preaching of the Gospel have seen real community transformation, but Richard has.

This incredible book, "Sheltered by Jesus" tells how the Spirit of God has used The Skowhegan Miracle Shelter to bring Kingdom of God transformation to the town, region as well as greater and greater Gospel influence to the state.

Richard, being the visionary he is, has a vision that through ministry to the homeless by evangelical churches that revival will come to our churches and awakening to our nation. I believe this movement of churches ministering to the homeless will do just that. In the process, the same types of miracles that Richard's Gospel centered ministry has experienced will sweep our nation as well as Jesus vindicates the bold, sacrificial preaching of Gospel to the "least of these."

— *Dr. Ves A. Sheely*
District Superintendent of New England District of EFCA

This book and its author will demonstrate that God is working all things together for His good will and He can do the same for you if you earnestly seek and follow Him. Having been with Richard on this journey from its genesis I have witnessed miracle after miracle after miracle…because Richard is just crazy enough to believe that God is God. As Pastor likes to say, "He's not the Great I Was….He's the Great I AM," and may this book lead you on a path to experience the "Great I AM" in new and exciting ways.

— *Ron Spaulding*

The New Testament is filled with miracles that recount not just what Jesus did but what He does. I say does, because He is alive and at work at the shelter in Skowhegan! His presence and power are real there because of the childlike faith and fearless love for the broken and hurting that Pastor Berry and friends at Trinity EFC model so humbly and faithfully for us. The stories in this book will reignite your walk with God.

—*Gary G. Hoag, Ph.D.*
EFCA Church Liaison and
Visiting Professor at Trinity Evangelical Divinity School

Sheltered by Jesus

SHELTERED by Jesus

A Voice for the Homeless

RICHARD BERRY

Sheltered By Jesus
A Voice for the Homeless

All stories detailed herein are factual; however, certain names of individuals and companies have been omitted or reduced in order to protect the identity of these persons or companies.

ISBN: 978-0-911802-86-3
Kindle edition
ISBN: 978-0-911802-87-0

Published in the United States of America
Published by
NextStep Resources
7890 12th Ave South Minneapolis, MN 55425
(800) 444-2665
Design, Layout and Format: Kim Gardell, Graphic Design

Proceeds from the sale of this book go to support the ministry of the Skowhegan Homeless Shelter

DEDICATION

I would like to dedicate this book to my wife, Selma (Merry) Berry. She has always been there, encouraging me to try to do things I did not believe I was capable of doing. She has had more faith in me than I've had in myself. Jesus used her to inspire me to step out and attempt what I believed was the impossible. In my opinion, the toughest job in the world is to be a pastor's wife. They suffer silently when their husband is crying behind closed doors. Without her and Jesus, none of this would have been possible. The Lord gave Eve to Adam because He knew she was what he needed. He gave Selma to me for the exact same reason, only she did not lead me astray, but instead kept me moving forward when I would have given up. I pray that all pastors would be blessed with a true helper as God has blessed me.

ACKNOWLEDGMENTS

I want to say a special thank you to my daughter Denise Wood for typing my book and my Granddaughter Kaitlin Wood for helping with the editing along with my wife Selma.

A special thanks to the staff without which the shelter would not be able to operate.

Thanks to all who gave of their time, materials and finances to build and operate this shelter.

About the photos on the cover:

The *man on the cover* was nicknamed "Spike." After trying to live under a carport, he came to the shelter with his hair and beard covered in ice. He lost some toes to diabetes and gangrene and eventually had to be placed in a nursing home. His condition worsened to the point of requiring a leg amputation, but having been through so much trauma in his life already, he refused the operation and succumbed to his ailments. We praise God that he is now sheltered by Jesus for eternity.

The *baptismal* was a gift from Jeff Hodges, a friend who heard me speak at his home church in Wethersfield, CT. He once faced the possibility of homelessness and wanted the homeless in our shelter to have a special place to be baptized. Prior to this, we were using a horse watering trough. What a difference!

The *rock cross* was built by a young homeless man who wished to give back to the shelter. He thought he didn't have much to offer, but all who enter the park behind the shelter see this monument, and it has become very precious to our staff and residents.

TABLE OF CONTENTS

FOREWORD

I was first introduced to the ministry of Trinity Homeless Shelter in November of 2011 when my dear Aunt and Uncle sent me a CD of a message delivered by Pastor Richard Berry at their church in Connecticut. The date on this CD was the Sunday after Thanksgiving.

Just four days earlier, our church board went through the painful ordeal of losing our building, and we were about to lose the parsonage as well. I had returned from a meeting at the bank to break the news to my wife that we were now a "homeless" congregation and that we would soon have no place to live, either. It was the day before Thanksgiving, 2011. There was nothing happy about it and we certainly didn't feel very thankful.

The process of losing our building included showing it to potential buyers. Three other church groups expressed interest and came to look at our facility. I met with each one personally to make sure they understood that we did not want to sell our building, but were out of options.

I was about to learn an important lesson about organized religion and the traditional church model in America.

Surrounded by religious leaders and church representatives, not one offered to pray for me. No one put their hand on my shoulder and spoke words of encouragement to me. No one even said they were sorry we were going through this difficult time. No one offered their building to us so that we could continue to worship together as a church family. It seemed as if our demise meant less competition in the complex world of "kingdom business." We were just another sad story in the ongoing saga of the "Great Recession" of our time.

While these prospective buyers were busy planning their expansions and developing their outreach programs, I was a wounded fish in a vast ocean and the sharks were starting to circle me. I had failed; I was overwhelmed and powerless, and never felt more alone. What I thought my church needed was a financial miracle. What my church got instead was a CD in the mail.

After relocating my spacious church office (complete with a private bathroom and walk-in closet) into the crowded, window-less basement of the parsonage, still unsure of how long we would even be living there, I listened to that CD – not once, but three consecutive times. I wept all three times and thought if God will do this for a pastor in Maine, then surely He would do something for me, a pastor in Illinois. I decided to reach out to Pastor Berry and talk to him personally.

The stories he shared about Trinity Homeless Shelter and the encouragement he freely gave began to restore my hope with every phone call, and just as important, to challenge my own perspectives.

Something amazing started to happen. It had nothing to do with planning sessions, program budgets, buildings and attendance; it had to do with me. I was no longer angry and disillusioned. Although wounded, I no longer felt betrayed. Instead, I was able to identify my own shortcomings and the spiritual shallowness of some of my ministry beliefs.

When Pastor Berry told me that the homeless were praying for me every single day, I was humbled beyond words, and began to believe that God did not abandon me, that He really did have an assignment for me, and I was in this "business" (whatever this business was) because He called me to it.

The following year, my Aunt and Uncle told me Pastor Berry would be speaking at their church again. We drove a thousand miles to meet this man and to hear his story in person. Pastor Berry greeted me with a warm embrace, encouraging words, and a reminder that the homeless were continually praying for me, by name, every single day. I sat through the service with my family and wept again.

Pastor Berry and I have since become friends and I am honored and privileged to offer the following thoughts about the ministry of Trinity Homeless Shelter and to brag a little about my friend.

First, I am most impressed with Pastor Berry's intimacy with his "Daddy," God. What might be considered insignificant is actually the greatest need in the Body of Christ today, specifically among God's pastors and leaders—to know Him as Daddy. If we are to be the leaders He needs us to be, then we must make it our business to pursue intimacy first and foremost. It's easy to manifest the love and compassion of a God you know and experience intimately.

Second, his simple, yet profound faith in God sets him apart as a man who actually expects his prayers to be answered. Prayer is more than a formal, public display lacking any real power. This is another example he sets for others to follow.

Third, I have never once heard him say, "look at the ministry we've built" or "look at the exciting new programs we've developed." Pastor Berry continues to boldly boast in our Daddy-God and what He is doing. That's what these stories are all about—the love of our Father God.

Finally, I've long maintained that there are no denominational neighborhoods in heaven and lamented that the church has set a terrible example of true love and unity here on the earth. If we believe that we're all one by our faith in the Lord Jesus Christ, why do we continue to cultivate and maintain our own "brand" of Christianity?

Pastor Rich Berry doesn't seem to care much about the different labels we go by, and that is why I believe God has raised him up and given him a voice to help lead the way back to a demonstration of love and unity.

I remain a partner with compassionate love through the ministry of Trinity Homeless Shelter. I pray that God will use this book to convince us to stop pursuing cultural relevance, with all the bells and whistles, and start being the relevance. I have yet to hear Pastor Berry tell the church we must all build homeless shelters; rather, we must all be about the business of simply loving and caring for people.

I've heard him say it many times before, but I want to say it again for him: JESUS CHRIST DID NOT DIE FOR A SINGLE PROGRAM OR BUILDING. HE DIED FOR PEOPLE.

May God help us to come back to the simplicity of loving people.

— *Rev. Gary J. Cortese, Jr.*,
Pastor, Global Harvest Church, Byron, Illinois
November 2015

CHAPTER 1

My friend Mike said to me, "I am going to be homeless this Friday at noon! What are you going to do about it, Pastor Berry?" Talk about life changing moments! My Christian life, and my future time in ministry, was headed for a drastic change as I had no idea what to say to him at that moment. Little did I know that right then it was actually Jesus asking me "Are you ready for some miracles?"

For 18 years Mike and I traveled together many times officiating ball games together. I would share the love of Christ with him and invite him to church. He always had an excuse at the last moment. But Jesus was preparing to do away with excuses for both of us.

I had been ministering in a small church in Skowhegan, Maine, the one in which I had come to Christ in 1977, the same year they built the church. I was 29 years old at the time and wanted nothing to do with church until then.

I got married May 30, 1970, to my wife Selma. She was an immature believer who did not know she shouldn't marry an unbeliever. I believe the miracles began then with God bringing us together knowing I would become a believer and what He was planning to do with me. My wife and her grandmother prayed for my salvation for seven years. The day I received Jesus, things began to happen in my life. Six months later, I felt the call to ministry and it was so strong I cried out to Jesus to make a way for me to go to Bible school and into the ministry. I had two strikes against me. #1 I was a lousy student, and #2 I had three small children and a pile of bills. I cried out to Jesus and said, "I do not care what you have to do so I can go to school." The miracles were about to start. But before the miracles at the homeless shelter, Jesus did a major one in answer to my prayer.

In April of 1980 when I cried out to God, I was working as a logger in the woods with my dad, Robert Berry, and my brother Edward Berry. A logger is someone who cuts trees in the forest and hauls them out to go to mills that make lumber or paper. That's what I grew up doing, and my dad was a logger his entire life. On this particular day, I was sitting on the front of the skidder, a large tractor used to haul the logs, and Dad was pushing the logs onto the pile with the blade on the front of the skidder. I looked away for a split second and Dad hit the lever. The blade came up and caught my left foot and crushed it. Some would call it an accident, but I knew then and truly know today, that it was the first of many answered prayers to get me to school and in 28 years get me to the place where Mike would ask for help.

CHAPTER 2

WHEN MIKE ASKED me what I would do, I froze. What a sad commentary of a pastor with 25 years in the ministry — I had no idea how to help. What was I going to do? I had taught the story of the Good Samaritan many times, but now the question was, "Am I that man?"

I also knew my church and how we operated, just like most churches. A situation comes up and you're supposed to go to the church with a special business meeting to form a committee to report back to the church for a decision. Big problem! Mike needs an answer now! My response, "I have a couch in the counseling room where you can stay, but you *cannot tell anyone*!" The battles and miracles were now on the way. My ministry was changed forever at that exact moment.

Three months prior to Mike coming to me, I had triple-bypass surgery. I had been taking care of the wood for the outside wood boilers that heated the church, and also cleaned the church when no one volunteered. Now, Mike offered to do that for allowing him to stay at the church. A couple of weeks passed and some individuals would come to me and say how amazed they were that a man who never was in church was now there an awful lot! I answered "Yeah, he is," but, I knew the cat was out of the bag, so I called a special business meeting to tell the church what I had done.

The meeting came and I was really afraid of how it would go. I had broken the rules of the church, and some members were sticklers for proper procedure. But I saw the hand of God move in that meeting. I asked for more folks than just Mike to be allowed to stay there. I asked to put bunk beds in a classroom and to start allowing some homeless to stay at the church. The reason being I had been involved in a jail ministry for the past year and many were coming to Jesus. They had the same question as Mike, "We have no place to go when we get out, so what are *you* going to do about that? " Again, I felt for them, but didn't have a clue.

They had said to me "You said if we accepted Jesus, our sins would be forgiven, we would be righteous in God's eyes and brothers with Christ and you. Is that true?" I replied that it was the truth. So now they said "Jesus does not want us to commit any more crimes, but when we are released in the winter and have no clothes, food, or home, what are we supposed to do?" You know, God has a way of putting that mirror right in your face and asking "Well, what are you going to do?" So now, I asked my church to allow these new believers to come and stay at the church until they could take care of themselves. I truly believed they would vote "No" and it would all end right there. I could then, with a clear conscience, tell everyone, "Sorry, but my church will not allow it." Not my problem! But I was blown away when they voted "yes" by 100% vote! Talk about the power of God! I just witnessed the Red Sea opening and Lazarus raised from the dead, all in one swift swoop.

CHAPTER 3

THE WORD TRAVELED fast that we were taking in the homeless and the numbers grew fast. Soon, we were making more beds and filling up more rooms. This began to make many of the church members uncomfortable, as many of the men coming in off the street had just been released from jail. I was amazed at how many desired to come and live in a church.

The influx of new believers with checkered pasts was not easy for many church members to take. I remember being asked to come over to one young family's home for a visit, a very nice family that I was close to and that truly loved me as their pastor and friend. I had watched their children grow up and even officiated many games they played in at school. When I arrived, they started the conversation with "We want you to know we love you and respect you and truly believe you are doing what God has called you to do. But, we can no longer go to church with those kind of people. They make us nervous and even smoke outside the church building."

I guess I was naive, because I was caught off guard by what I was hearing. To hear the phrase "those kind of people" hurt my heart. All I could think of at the moment was Jesus being accused of hanging out with sinners. I had expected a "no vote" from the congregation, but was totally unprepared for these words from this family. I felt like a mule kicked me in the guts! It really hurt to hear those words. As I was leaving, each one came over and hugged me and reassured me of their love for me as a pastor and friend. I left that night feeling hurt, but not realizing that this would be the sentiment of the majority of my church family.

The massive exodus had begun. Over a period of six months, 80% of the congregation left. As one of the leaders in the church was leaving, he shared this thought with me. "Everyone is taking their checkbooks with them, so you won't be able to pay the bills, and the church building will be repossessed. How will you house them then? You have just destroyed a church to care for *them*!"

CHAPTER 4

I WENT HOME, sat on the foot of my bed, raised my hands into the air and began to cry out to the Lord. I asked Him if I had misread the leading of the Holy Spirit by taking in the homeless. I said, "If you are not behind this, I have destroyed a church and put the homeless back on the street." I pleaded for a clear answer so as to know where to go from here. What I got was not what I expected.

God brought the story of Gideon (Judges 7) to my mind. If you read the story you will see how God told Gideon that he could not defeat the huge army of the Midianites because he had too many warriors. As those images raced through my mind, all I could say to God was, "Wow!" So I read the account of Gideon again and saw God shrink his army from thirty-two thousand to three hundred men. God told Gideon, and I truly believe that He told me as well, "I will give you victory in battle after I shrink your army to a size that you could never boast about how you and your army accomplished anything." That day, I got it!

I prepared to preach a message to my church that I never dreamed I would preach. I told them the account of Gideon and that I believed God was telling me the same thing. I was prepared to stand with Jesus if it meant He would be all that was left with me and the homeless, and I did not "give a rat's behind" if I stood alone and lost it all and had to turn off the lights on my way out for the last time. Little did I know that day what God had in store for this dumb hick pastor and a tiny church in a place called Skowhegan, Maine. I was about to begin living the things I'd been reading and teaching about Israel and the early church with all those miracles that I did not believe happens today in the present church. For the very first time in my ministry and Christian life, I could not survive without miracles.

The miracles started with monies coming in to pay the bills. No way were we going to survive on 18 people putting money in an offering plate! As word got out that we were having homeless people inside a church building, calls began coming for interviews. Local papers and TV stations came to interview me and the residents. They were amazed to see my classrooms with bunk beds in them. Soon, some magazines called and wanted to run articles on the shelter. People all over the country began to respond and I was blown away when I opened the mailbox and saw addresses from Maine to California with checks in them. Every time a bill would come due some checks would show up. We never had an unpaid bill and never had a clue from where the money would come. I slowly came to the place where

I expected all needs to be met. The residents were required to attend daily morning prayers and Bible studies. I watched them grow, like Miracle Grow had been spread on them, and pray expecting God to answer as they saw the miracles.

Now, as the numbers began to grow, so did the need for more of everything, especially food. As it just so happens, my nephew was the manager of a local food chain market. He got them to give us produce that was near the end of its shelf life. A bakery began donating breads and sweets that had been taken off the store shelves. Between the two, we were able to feed those living in the church as well as open a food pantry for some local folks whose cupboards began to get bare by the end of the month until food stamps came out again. It's tough to describe the looks on their faces when they fill up a box and know they will make it through another month because our shelter was there.

That first year there were times when things would get pretty tight, but I have to say I was getting fairly comfortable with the ministry. I also spoke at a couple of local churches and received some help with monies, toiletries, and clothing. It was actually getting kind of exciting to see souls saved and needs met by Jesus!

CHAPTER 5

SOME INTERESTING RESIDENTS showed up, and one in particular had a huge impact on me. I received a phone call from the social services at the local hospital. The man asked if it was true that I was allowing people to stay in my church. I informed him that it was true. He said "Now that's amazing, Pastor Berry. I have a gentleman here who goes by the name of Reno. He is 74 years old. He was living on the streets, had a heart attack, and was found lying on a snow bank. He was revived and brought here. We later learned he's had several minor attacks and is not in very good condition. We have done all we can and he is to be released from the hospital. We offered to pay for a room at a local motel, but he's afraid to be alone so does not want to live there. He is clutching a newspaper article about you and said he wants to go live with you. Will you take him?" I told him I would and we'd come and pick him up ourselves. When we arrived I saw an old man, totally worn out, standing about five feet tall, and scared to death he was going to die.

Reno came to my office shortly after he arrived and shared his story with me. He was thrown out of his home when he was 16 years old. His parents said they did not want him. He had been married and divorced three times and what family he had lived in Texas and wanted nothing to do with him. So he said, "I am 74 years old, alone, and scared. I need a home and a family that loves me." He became a sort of mascot around the shelter and seemed to have finally found a family. He came to me one day and shocked me by asking if my wife and I would adopt him and be his mom and dad. I had shared how I had adopted my son and now he decided he wanted to be my son as well. Now, what do you say to a little old man who wants a family and picks you? I said, "No! I love you, Reno, but I am not going to adopt you!" He really took it hard and then asked if he could call me "Dad" and my wife "Mom," since he felt as though he never had parents. We both agreed, and it became a source of laughter around the shelter and church when they would hear him call out "Hi, Mom. Hi, Dad."

Later on, Reno needed a triple-bypass surgery to clear up blockages. We went to visit him at the hospital, and when we entered the room, he cried out "Hi, Mom and Dad!" I cannot do justice to the expression on his nurse's face, and again, when I answered, "Hi, Son." The nurse approached us when we left his room and asked, "You are not his parents, are you? It's obvious he's older than either of you." We shared the story with her and when we came to visit again, the nurse called to him, "Your mom and dad are here."

Those are the precious moments you cling to when the battles come, and one was on the way. A storm was brewing and I did not even know it. I knew some of my neighbors were not excited about having homeless living next to them, and they had not been afraid to voice their opinions with me. But that hadn't risen to any significant degree. What I was not aware of was the Police Chief did not want my ministry in his town and a plot was already underway.

CHAPTER 6

I REMEMBER THE day as though it was yesterday when the Code Enforcement Officer paid me a visit. I was sharing lunch with some residents in the kitchen of the shelter when he arrived. His words were, "I've been sent here by the Chief of Police and told to find a way to shut you down." I was thrown for a loop, and my first thought was, "Why?" All I'm trying to do is help hurting people, so why am I now an enemy of the police? He went on to explain to me that I was not coded to be a homeless shelter. My response was, "I'm not a homeless shelter. I am simply a church with beds in it." He didn't seem to agree with me so I explained my answer further. I said, "I've had church groups come and spend the nights in my church in the past. The only difference is these ones stayed!" I guess I am just a dumb hick from Skowhegan, because I believed what I said. I truly did not know I couldn't let people stay in the church.

So we proceeded to examine my church, and he pointed out code violations. There were quite a few and he warned me that the State Fire Marshall would probably add to the list. At that moment, I was extremely confused as I believed God called me to do this, so why wasn't he protecting me? I was about to get some lessons on how God works things out for His glory and how He likes to "show off." I have since shared how Jesus looked for the "dumbest man in America", because that is how He gets the greatest glory. I was too dumb to understand, and just dumb enough to trust Him and move ahead. So I went home, sat on the foot of my bed, raised my hands toward Heaven, prayed, and cried like a baby. I was never one to cry over much of anything, but that was about to change dramatically.

The next day, I called the Chief and asked to meet with him. I had never met him until this point in time. He agreed to meet with me that morning. As I entered his office I introduced myself and he couldn't be described as anything close to pleasant, to say the least. I said, "I heard you are trying to shut me down. Is that true?" He said, "Yes, and you are the worst thing ever to happen to Skowhegan." All this time, he was pointing his finger at me and the look on his face told me he'd like to be ripping mine off! I could not grasp what he was saying, because all I was attempting to do was house and feed homeless people. But he had the same problem as those who left my church because they did not desire to be around "those kind of people." All I could do was say "Have a nice day" and walk away. As I was leaving he informed me to prepare myself for an onslaught of visits from state fire marshals, the local fire chief, and code enforcement. I left with no delusion of how he felt about me and the mission God called me to do. The battles had just begun, and I was beginning to learn how to pray like never before.

It did not take long for the Chief's threats to come to fruition. One day some cars came to the church and out stepped the State Fire Marshall, local Fire Chief, and the Code Enforcement Officer. They informed me that they were there to investigate code violations and began to go through my church and did not miss a spot. By the time their investigation had ended, they had three and a half pages of violations that had to come into compliance or I'd be shut down. I went over the list and some things we could fix, but some, such as a sprinkler system and larger windows that would mean cutting up brick walls to install were out of the church's financial abilities to do. We now only had 18 nonresidents and were depending on outside funding to keep us afloat at the time. So, this "brave man" of "great faith" found himself back on the foot of the bed, hands in the air, praying and crying like some baby.

You know it's embarrassing when you hear people applaud you for your faith and strength and courage when you know none of it fits! Wow, can you imagine some were comparing me to Joshua because of my great faith? They would make statements like, "Just like Joshua stepped into the Jordan River by faith, you stepped out to help the homeless by faith." No, I did not! Joshua entered Jordan on his own; Jesus picked me up and threw me in! I did not know how to respond to a friend who was going to be homeless and I had run my mouth about the love of Christ to him and now I was "forced" to back it up. Jesus stuck me in a corner and wouldn't let me out. Wow, some great man of faith!

CHAPTER 7

WHILE I AM trying to figure out how to keep the shelter open until springtime, Jesus brings more "special people" to the shelter to show me it must continue.

I got a call from the jail on a Friday night. The officer explained how an 84 year old man had been brought in for domestic violence against his wife. He explained how the wife suffered from Alzheimer's and everyone knew the violence claim was not true. But it's Friday night and there is no way to get him before a judge to get him released. The officer said the old man had no idea what was going on because he was in the early stages of Alzheimer's himself. The officer pleaded with me to take him. He even offered to deliver him to the shelter. I told him I'd take him. I was amazed to find out more about this man the next day. He was a highly decorated soldier during WWII. He received the Belgian Cross for going into a Nazi death camp and leading prisoners out by the hand. The other thing of which they were not aware was that he was incontinent. Jesus showed me just how special a place He was raising up. The residents found out he was a war hero and they took care of him. They changed his clothes, cleaned his messes, showered him, made his bed, and brought his meals to him in bed. Jesus showed me what "those kind of people" could do when shown the love of Jesus. They poured that love out on this special old veteran. He stayed two weeks and then was allowed to live at the Veteran's Home in Togus, Maine. I could hear Jesus asking me, "Son, is this worthy of a few battles?" I cried out, "I get it. I'll stay in the fight!"

CHAPTER 8

SHORTLY AFTER THE visit by those who inspected my facility, I got the call that a meeting had been called for me to address my situation. It was to be held in the town office building in Skowhegan. The day the meeting was to take place it was 25 degrees below zero with the wind chill factor. It was even snowing outside, but it sure was even "colder" on the inside at the meeting!

I've read Acts Chapter 4 many times and knew very well the story of Peter and John before the Sanhedrin (ruling Jewish Committee), but now I was going to experience something very similar myself.

Prior to leaving for the meeting, all the residents asked to sit in on the meeting. There was an area for any audience and there they sat with their lives on the line. Today would determine if they would be warm and fed or cold and hungry, hopelessly wandering the streets. Believe me when I say that there was great fervor in the prayers that morning prior to leaving for the meeting. There was a huge measure of hope and fear all wrapped up in one.

When I sat at the conference table, there was me, all alone, facing a team made up of state fire marshals, a code enforcement officer, Police Chief, and Town Selectmen. If you don't think I was praying you would be crazy. But what happened next totally amazed me. Jesus took over, and my spirit quieted and I was suddenly set to take them on. I looked across at those homeless faces and knew Jesus had not brought us this far to put them out on the street in subzero weather and a snow storm.

The Chief of Police was literally shaking as he asked to go first to question me. The more he shook the calmer I got, and it blew my mind.

Chief: You claim to have a rule that does not permit residents on the streets after 9pm. My officers have returned some of your residents after 9pm. If you truly have these rules as you claim, we should never see them off property after 9pm, should we?

Me: Chief, you have a great police force and I see them out and about all the time. But, I guess I am a little confused. The street on which I live has a sign that says '35 miles per hour.' You have a clearly defined rule that all can see. But I see blue lights come on, and cars pulled over, and tickets written for speeding. Is that not true? How can that be since you have a rule and it's clearly posted? We both know people break the rules at times. We can't prevent that and would be foolish to think we could. So you write a speeding ticket and they pay the price for breaking the rules. I operate the same way. One of two things happen when people are caught out after 9pm. One is they are asked to leave and the other is what we call house arrest where they cannot be off the property at any time unless accompanied by a member of my staff.

The Chief literally hung his head but then said he had another question.

Chief: You claim to have zero tolerance for drugs and alcohol, but I know that a search was made by a probation officer who discovered drugs hidden in a mattress. (He turned to the probation officer and asked if that was not correct. He stated it was true.) So then, Pastor Berry, what do you have to say to that?

Again, he was shaking because he was so angry.

Me: Yes, Chief, that is the truth. But, may I ask you a question? Doesn't the jail have bars and guards and detectors to prevent drugs from entering the jail?"

Chief: Yes, that's true.

Me: Well, is it also true they have had inmates overdose on drugs while in jail? (He admitted it was.) So, why would I ever believe it to be impossible to sneak drugs into my church building where I have none of these things?

Once again he hung his head and that ended his questions.

Jesus won! As soon as the Chief was done, the Fire Marshall spoke up. He said, "Those things are not the issue for which I am here. Pastor Berry, how are you going to address the problem of code violations? I am responsible for the safety of those residents." I told him I was also. So I asked him, "Are they not safer in my building than in a car turned orange inside by fumes from propane heaters? Are they not safer in subzero weather in my church than between buildings or on park benches? Look at those people in the audience. They are residents here today to hear their fate. The town is broke and can't afford to pay for housing. The state is broke and can't offer vouchers for homes at this time. I'm their only option, so please tell me what I have to do to keep them in my church and off the streets."

The Fire Marshall looked at me and proclaimed, "You need to build a new shelter that is up to code as you can't bring your current building to code." I replied, "Okay." He asked me, "How are you going to do that?" I replied, "I have no idea! But, I will do whatever it takes to keep from sending these people out onto the streets." To that he replied,

"Show me progress and I will let you keep them in your church until the new shelter is built."

Then I saw Jesus start to do something amazing that I will never forget. I walked up to the Chief and put my arm around his neck and pulled him up close to me. The look on his face was precious! I said to him (and I know it was the Holy Spirit speaking), "Chief, I'm disappointed in you." He looked bewildered and asked why. I said, "Every Saturday evening I have a service at the church and I'm surrounded by 'those kind of people' and you don't show up to protect me." He looked at me and started to laugh and then said to me "Pastor Berry, I want you to know this is not about you. I see you as a man of honesty and integrity. I simply don't want those people in my town." Our relationship began to improve at that moment. The Chief never did attend one of my church services, but I won't be surprised one day if he shows up at my shelter and proclaims he gave his life to Jesus. He has since moved on to another job and I can truly say our relationship grew to the place that I miss him. I watched the power of the Holy Spirit turn that man from being my enemy to becoming my friend in the end.

CHAPTER 9

WELL, THE DAY I left that meeting I spoke to Jake, an old stubborn German, who was a retired building engineer. He had started attending my church because of an article in the local paper that told about a church with people living in it. He was in a Bible study group that had saved some money and asked God to show them a ministry with which they could share. The article came out the next morning after they prayed. The heading was "Prayers Answered!" They believed that was their answer. He and his wife came to church and stayed. So, I approached Jake and asked him to head up this building project, as I couldn't even build a knob for an old outhouse.

He said he would do it and asked, "How much money do you have to get started?" I simply replied, "None." He said that sounded very interesting, to say the least. I said, "Jake, we need to show progress on the building with no money and no equipment or materials." He said, "Come on and we'll make some progress." He proceeded to get four stakes and we went out back of the church and measured off what we figured would be the size of this new building. He drove four corner stakes into the ground, stood back and proudly declared, "Pastor Berry, that's your new homeless shelter." "That's a corker" (Richard Berry's hick language for "That's awesome"), I replied. He then took out his camera and took a picture of the four stakes. We mailed it to the State Fire Marshall's office, and their reply was "That's progress." Jesus has a sense of humor! Now, people took this as if I had great faith and could see a building standing there. The truth is that old German did, because he had greater faith than I did. I spent too many years preaching miracles were for the Nation of Israel in the Old Testament and the Apostolic Age in the early church. This dumb old hick from Skowhegan was thinking, "There, this will hold them off until spring before they shut me down." Not exactly Abraham, Joshua, or Paul! But Jesus was about to change my thinking and build my faith to the place of expectation.

A couple of days later I was at a local convenience store and saw a man I hadn't seen in years. It was Ned Goff, the salesman who sold a skidder to my dad. (A skidder is a large tractor to use in the logging business.) That was back in 1969, just after I got out of the Navy. He approached me and asked how I'd been and what I was doing these days. I learned he had started his own business since I last saw him. He now owned an equipment rental business called Skowhegan Rental. I went on to explain how I had started a homeless shelter and had people living in my church, and the battle I was facing due to code violations. He listened intently and then asked how much money I had for this new project. I then explained that I simply had no funds whatsoever. He asked what I had for equipment to build such a building. Again, I shared how I had none. I told him I did have four stakes in the ground and "had to borrow them from Jake." He roared with laughter as he looked at me like I had an eye in the middle of my forehead. Little did I know that when he finished laughing I would experience my first of many miracles. All of a sudden, he got very serious and said to me "I'll tell you what. When you are ready to begin, call me and you can have any equipment you need and it will all be for free." I couldn't believe it! I felt like Moses standing at the Red Sea with Pharaoh's army closing in fast, and all of a sudden the waters parted so he can walk through on dry ground. Maybe, just maybe, I was wrong all these years. Maybe Jesus is the Great I Am and not the Great I Was! Could it be that God was going to use this dumb hick who sat crying like a baby on his bed to show off His glory today as He did in the past? Wow!

I went home and began what would become a daily ritual of walking around the stakes with my hands raised toward heaven, praising God for what He'd already done, and praying for the building to grow.

First we needed to dig out for the foundation. I called my friend and the heavy equipment was delivered. I was then blessed to learn one of the men on my staff was an operator—of course! So he dug the huge hole for the foundation. Now I had four stakes and a huge hole in the ground. I named it the Holy of Holes after the Holy of Holies in the Jerusalem Temple. It is amazing how God can use a simple hole in the ground to glorify Himself and lift my spirits. I was really proud of that hole! Sounds kind of weird now, but it didn't at the time. I was so overwhelmed that God had done this in support of the homeless. Things were actually underway in spite of my disbelief that God did such things today.

One morning we had a surprise visitor in the Holy of Holes. Some of the men came running to me saying, "Come quick and see this." When I arrived I saw a little black animal with a white stripe down its back—a little skunk! It had climbed down into the six foot hole but could not get back out. Its claw prints were on the side of the walls of the hole. There he was, all exhausted from spending the night attempting to escape what was now a prison for him. Once again, Jesus would give me a lesson on how sweet the hearts were of these homeless men. God allowed them a few moments to get their minds off themselves and onto this scared little animal. They begged me, "Pastor, please don't hurt him." I guess they were afraid I'd turn into Attila the Hun or something. My heart was blessed over what happened next. Some of the men took a blanket over to the skunk, without any forethought that he would spray them, and that they would then spend the night outside. That would've been the natural thing for him to do to them. But I believe Jesus brought a calmness to him so that he somehow understood they intended to help him. To my utter amazement they were able to wrap him up and carry him out of that deep hole and he never sprayed once! Now perhaps you would not call that a miracle, but don't attempt to change the minds of those homeless men and this dumb ol' Pastor. We all gave thanks as if Jesus had just sent manna from heaven.

I guess God figured I needed a "faith boost" so He showed me He was all over this project. We were getting ready to run water lines to the future building as they needed to go in prior to the building going up. Jake came to me and said, "Pastor, we've gone as far with this as we can unless we get some actual money. The water company will not come in with pipe unless they get paid up front. We asked if we could pay in installments and got turned down." I asked how much and he said $1,800. May as well have been $18 million. But, as we were talking the mail came in and I headed to the mailbox with Jake at my side. There was a letter inside from an Evangelical Free Church in Vermont. The letter read, "We took up a love offering and it was really small and I would've been embarrassed to send that amount, but someone came along and added a large donation." The check came in at $2,000. I handed it to Jake and said "OK, go get the water lines." We both stood there for a moment blown away by the timing as well as the amount of the check. Jesus knew when and how much was needed and it showed up just in time. Jesus never gave us a huge surplus but as we kept praying He gave us all we needed.

CHAPTER 10

IT SEEMED LIKE as we waited, Jesus' plan was to boost our faith with a few miracles. I sure feel foolish today as a pastor for not believing and trusting Jesus to perform miracles today when needed. Sometimes I feel like I should've been named Peter, not because I am the rock (meaning of the Greek word πέτρος which is Peter), but instead for continually doubting and putting my big foot in my mouth like Peter was accustomed to doing.

I remember well one day when a new man came to the shelter. The one thing he desired more than anything was to take a shower. I agreed it was of major importance at the time. It had definitely been a while since any soap and water had flowed over that body! I told him to sign in, and the staff member would issue what he needed for toiletries and a towel. He soon came back into my office and explained we just ran out. So I talked to Jesus about that. How can I run a shelter with no towels and no money to buy any? The staff member offered to give him one of his for which I was eternally grateful!

Now I lived in the parsonage next to the church and started walking to my home when I saw three large boxes on my front steps. UPS had delivered them from an address in Maryland. I looked at the name of the sender and had never heard of this person before. So I opened the boxes and lo and behold they were filled with new towels from J.C. Penney in Maryland. "I don't believe it," I said. "He did it to me again." I was never out of towels; I just thought I was, as they were on my steps when I needed them. I had to know how this all came together, so I called the telephone number from the address. A lady answered and I told her who I was. I said, "I'm Pastor Berry and I run the homeless shelter in Skowhegan, Maine. I have to know why you sent towels to the shelter in the first place." Once again, it was a "Jesus story." Her friend subscribes to the *Christian Science Monitor*. A writer for the magazine had written an article on me and the shelter. I remember it well because I laughed at the idea of this magazine doing an article on an evangelical church and Pastor. I truly thought "this is a total waste of my time," but I went along and did the interview. Well, that lady shared it with her friend who was so moved by it she said, "I knew I had to do something, but did not know what to do." Her friend then suggested the towels and she called J.C. Penney and had them deliver those three boxes. I told her they arrived at the exact moment I needed them. She was pleased and I ended up crying again. Do you see a pattern developing? Now my faith was beginning to grow, but that did not eliminate the crying. But I was determined He wouldn't surprise me again, which proved I hadn't yet learned all that much.

God is bringing things together with the building while these miracles continued on the side. We have a hole and now we need a foundation. Again I have a need and no money. I'd better get used to it, because it continued through the project for the most part. I would get some money at the right time but had none of our own. The man with the equipment asked where the cement was coming from and I gave my usual answer: "I have no idea!" He calls later and informs me he contacted some friends who would make a donation. The cement would all be FREE! Of course it would!

Then he asked me who was going to put up the forms for the cement and what I had for materials for the forms. I think he was getting the idea by now that I truly started this major project with no money and no idea how it would all come together. Remember now, I never believed it would happen in the first place. As it turns out, he had another friend who owed him a favor and he called in that favor. The man called me and told me he would bring the forms and put them up, but he needed laborers to help him as he couldn't hire a crew and do it for free. The homeless were about to embark on an opportunity to have a hand in the new home they and thousands to follow would enjoy. Since I have no skills at all, I simply did all I could to aid in the project. I walked around the project with hands toward heaven, praying. But now as I prayed, Jesus was teaching me to expect Him to do what I knew I couldn't. Like the Apostle Peter, I was now involved in on-the-job training with Jesus as the teacher.

Looking back I kind of relate where I was at the time to where Peter was early on in his walk with Jesus. I can truly relate to how Peter must have felt. In Matthew 14:25-31, Jesus comes out to the disciples on the lake while walking on water. I love what Peter does, because it helps me feel better when my faith is not up to snuff. Peter sees Him and asks Him to tell him to walk on the water. Jesus says to get out of the boat and walk. Amazing! Peter is dumb enough to do it, because we know we can't walk on water! But, lo and behold, he finds himself walking on water. He begins to sink. Why? It's simple—he knew he couldn't walk on water, and he was right. He couldn't! But Jesus could take him beyond what he could do by using a miracle. Then Jesus rubbed it in his face by reminding him of his lack of faith. I see us walking on water as we're building a shelter that we cannot build and needing to be dumb enough not to know it. Then our faith grows.

Just like Peter stepping out of the boat, God kept asking me to trust Him to do what I deemed impossible. The number of residents is rising, so along with needs for a building there was also the need for more heat in the winter as we were operating seven days per week with more rooms calling for heat. The light bills and water bills are growing because we are using the showers more, and the laundry is growing, resulting in even higher light and water bills. And as I look back, I am totally amazed how everything was paid and like Peter on the water, only Jesus knew how we stayed afloat.

The influx of numbers also meant a greater need for staffing. When we started, the staff was me and two others. Those days were now in the rear-view mirror. Again, it must be accomplished without any money. All staff members, including me, work as volunteers. The church continued to pay my salary with its meager offerings, but there were no salaries for the staff of the shelter.

Jesus began to give me a staff from amongst the homeless themselves. My original staff members were not homeless, so this was going to be a whole new challenge. You know what was tough is the fact I had never studied about how to run a homeless shelter out of a church with no money and no staff. And I even went to Bible school! So it became us and Jesus and on-the-job training like the early disciples experienced. No idea how it's going to get done, but simply see the need and move forward.

My staff began to come together one-by-one. I chose them as I saw potential to do a particular job needed, but did not see them with the ability to do anything alone. It became evident in a hurry that just because they were homeless did not mean they lost their knowledge and skills. So that was one criterion. The second was they were an example of following the rules outlined in the contract we had developed over time. It did not mean they were necessarily qualified to be an elder, deacon, etc. in the church. I was looking for those who could do a job and had both time and ability that I did not possess. The next requirement was they would work for room, board and some special privileges and amenities. I was shocked at how quickly residents asked to be considered for staff and began to take pride in helping others coming in as they were at one time. They have a heart for the homeless and you cannot put a price on that! People were amazed to hear some of their stories. Some come out of prison, some got divorced and walked away with only their clothes on their backs. Others had high paying jobs and lost them and could no longer pay a mortgage or car payment so they lost it all. Some arrive suicidal and find hope and more want to offer that to others in the same state. They come from tents or park benches or cars in a parking lot. But on staff, they regain their pride and dignity and that is worth more than money to many.

CHAPTER 11

TINKER WAS A great story of the power of transformations and reformation. He is now one of the members of one of my teams who travels to churches all over the country speaking. The man you see today does not even slightly resemble the one who appeared on my doorstep checking out the shelter.

One day this man appeared and I greeted him with a hug and a "welcome." He made my eyes water, but not because he was homeless. He and his wife, Amy, lived in the woods in a camper trailer with no power or running water. He asked if we had hot showers and I gleefully said, "Oh, Yes!" The odor was a killer! He hadn't had a haircut or shave in a long time and looked like the pictures of Big Foot. He had come to Jesus as a child but moved quite a distance away from Him over the years. He was battling depression, low self-esteem, drugs and alcohol. Jesus had his work cut out for him with this one.

When we got him cleaned up, we found out why he was called "Tinker." He could work on almost anything. He became a great asset to the shelter. Over a period of a few months, following a Saturday evening service, I asked to speak to him. He was quite nervous at first because it wasn't always a pleasant experience to be asked to see the Pastor if you were a resident. So he asked, "Did I do something wrong? I love it here and want to stay." I will have the following image in my mind for the rest of my life. I said, "Tinker, how would you like to be on my staff?" He literally fell to his knees, raised his hands toward heaven, and gave thanks. Can you imagine anyone that excited about working for room and board and a handful of privileges? His response caught me by surprise. He said "Thank you, Pastor! No one has ever shown me this kinds of respect and trust in my whole life! I will not let you down." And he hasn't.

This ministry is very unusual. It has so many battles and frustrations, but in the midst it all, there are these kind of moments. There were more of these types of stories to follow and some will be told later in this book.

CHAPTER 12

THROUGH ALL OF the stories of reformation, the building is still being erected. It was a privilege to see God's miracles in lives, as well as His providing supplies for the building.

Now that the crew is ready for cement and the forms were up, trucks began to show up and cement was flowing like a river into what would be the new foundation of the shelter. They put up frost walls and then before they could pour cement for the floor, sand and gravel was needed, so I prayed for both. Soon, six contractors volunteered to donate and deliver all that was needed—for free, of course!

I simply stood in awe as one company after another brought in the fill. I said, "Jesus, you are awesome!" I remember one of the men getting out of his truck and coming over to me. He said, "Pastor Berry, I almost didn't take part in this operation. The reason being is I didn't want to invest my time and money into something that would never get finished. Since you have no money and no idea where it's coming from, it seemed far-fetched to me that you would complete it. But, here

I am anyway." Of course he was! Jesus led him to go against common sense and take part in what seemed like a foolish endeavor, and if not for Jesus it would have been just that.

Once the fill was in and we were ready to pour the floor, Jake informed me that it could not snow for three weeks, until the cement was poured and hardened. Now understand that this is Maine in the winter and the chances of no snow would equal winning the Megabucks! So, once again, I walk around the site and pray. This time, for a miracle of no snow, and by the way, the weather channels all predicted large amounts of snow on the way. Now God had responded to a prayer by Joshua for something very similar. In Joshua 10:12-14, Joshua asked God to keep the sun from going down for one day over the area of Gibeon and he did. So Joshua won the battles and it says there never was a day like it since. I would like to add, until now! I have a witness to this, as a TV weather announcer on Channel 2 in Bangor, Maine, made this statement: "I do not have an explanation for this at all but there appears to be a 'bubble' over Central Maine. It is snowing all around that area, but none at all there." Wow! God wanted to boost my faith, and it sure was growing. Now the kicker! Jake comes to me and says, "The cement is done and now we need snow to cover it so it is insulated against the cold." Are you getting the picture? Yup!! I prayed and over the next few days a huge bed of snow fell and protected that floor perfectly. Of course He did!

Now it was time to begin building walls, but we had two problems: no money and no professional laborers. God continued to amaze and astound me as that evening Jake showed up at my door to inform me a friend of his showed up and told him their church just voted to give us $30,000 to get us started. He was almost speechless over it and I was in the same shape. The miracles are pouring in one after another. Faith Evangelical Free, our sister church, pastored by Bill Cripe decided to join forces with us. They added finances and I added simply a foolish belief that God would build this thing. That money went a long way, as donations of materials poured in as well. It became fun to watch Jesus weave all of this together.

So one problem was answered because we had some money, but what would we do about laborers? I prayed and it was as though God was not listening for the first time since we began. But God's answer was not the one I asked for or expected. The answer was to use the manpower within the men's shelter. I told Jake, "This is all we have to work with, so I guess you will have to train them and do the best you can." I look back on it and laugh, because poor ol' Jake had some frustrating days ahead. But I watched as men who could not drive a nail began to build and stand up the walls. Now it was very interesting at times. I remember one day in particular. Jake marked the base of the wall (I don't know what the correct term is.) and said, "Be sure to put the 2x6's on the right side of the mark." He said he had to leave for a while but there was no way to mess this up. Wrong! He returned to find them on the wrong side of the mark with two completed walls standing. The boys learned a lesson that day as they took down both walls and pulled every nail and stood the walls up again.

God has a great sense of humor—I am sure—and I bet he laughed louder than any of us as the men labored and Jake yelled. You see, this stubborn ol' German wanted perfection and was learning that the crew God gave him was anything but perfect. But, lo and behold, a building was taking form by the power of God and the work of a motley crew.

Now as the work progressed, God would send in professionals to volunteer their help. One man showed up one day and he didn't look like he could do anything, especially carpentry. He had been in an accident prior to this and had to have his face put back together. One eye was literally halfway down his face. I never saw anything like it. He proved to be an awesome carpenter and could see way better than I thought. In the past he had lost everything due to an alcohol problem and that also led to the accident. But he blamed himself and not God and wanted to help men who were where he was in the past, addicted, hopeless, and needing Jesus. He approached me one day and asked me "Do you know why I am here?" I replied, "Sure, to build a home for the homeless." I thought that was a "no brainer". But he said, "No, that's not entirely the reason I'm here." He had me curious now, so I asked him, "Why?" He told me God showed him in a vision that a revival was coming to America and was starting in Skowhegan, Maine with a homeless shelter. Sad to say, I blew it off and went home chuckling to myself, "Sure, God did." I had not believed in miracles for today and definitely not visions. I was inclined to ask him if he had eaten some bad pizza, but because he was a great carpenter, I kept my mouth shut. But, I never forgot what he had to say. Now I don't know where you stand on visions and miracles, and if you don't believe them, I understand why. I always believed that way, too. I learned all that in Bible School and taught it for 25 years.

As the building began to actually look like a building, others started to come forward and volunteer. I was amazed to be approached by Skowhegan High School's Shop Class. They offered to help with a set of stairs inside the building. It was so awesome to see these young people excited to have a hand in helping the homeless. This ministry was beginning to touch hearts outside our church and even outside Christian organizations.

You can't pray in the high school, but they came to a church for the homeless project. Jesus was taking this to places I didn't imagine it would go. The State of Maine even got in on the action. They contacted me to tell me the shelter was selected as the Crisis and Counseling Organization of the Year. They informed me that no other faith-based organization had ever received the award. I was asked to go to Augusta, the state capital, to receive the award. When I arrived, the head of the organization took me aside to speak to me privately.

He said, "I just wanted you to know that it was a battle to give you this award." Most stated their position, "We do not give a state organization award to a faith-based organization." He said, "I told them you were doing more this year than any of our organizations and there was no way you were not getting it!" I love it! Jesus got through and showed what He could do without a penny of taxpayers' money and no budget to work with—only faith and prayer and His power at work. My faith took another step forward that night as I saw Jesus glorified in front of people that did not want that to take place. This ministry was growing against all odds and being recognized for it, and I get to share in it firsthand. I'm not Joshua, but I feel like I'm watching the walls of Jericho falling, one by one! Praise the Lord!

Right after this, I received a letter and forms to fill out from the United Way. I was not aware of it, but they were giving $74,000 to homeless shelters in each county in Maine. Since I was the only one in Somerset County, they said the allotment was mine—simply fill out and return the forms. I was blown away and so excited. Yes, yes, yes! God had sent me the operating monies for the shelter. With a "homeless staff" working for room and board, and me volunteering with no salary, we could sustain the shelter and not even have to travel the country asking for funding. But I quickly learned that Satan can send a package that's pretty on the outside but a bomb on the inside. There was a catch in small print near the end of the contract. It stated you could not force anyone to attend church. They were living in my church! Duh!

Yes, they must attend church, and that's why we were seeing their lives change drastically. So I started saying as I traveled to speak, "We do not do it the 'United' way. We do it the Jesus way." Keep your money and your forms. I'll take Jesus every time.

Now I was told by my Pastor friend Bill Cripe that if I was going to make this work I would have to go outside the area and share this ministry. Because we were growing fast and the limited local donations wouldn't meet the needs of those living here and supply what was needed to build the new shelter. This ministry was overwhelming to start with, and now I was to carry it outside, plus run the shelter at the same time. All the while, the thoughts of "I am just a dumb hick from Skowhegan with only a three-year Bible school for an education" kept running through my mind. Most churches have men with Master's Degree and Doctorates from seminaries. How's an old Maine logger turned preacher supposed to get them to listen? I truly struggled with that from the very start of all of this. I'm in over my head and Jesus keeps moving out into deeper waters and tells me to keep on walking. I was truly getting sympathetic for Peter who realized he couldn't walk on water, even while he was doing it. But some crazy things were about to take place that would leave me speechless, and if you know me, that's sort of a miracle in itself.

CHAPTER 13

My nephew, Ron Spaulding, who is also an elder in my church, and I went to a prayer conference at Camp Spofford, a New England District Camp. The main speaker was Fritz Dale, who serves on the Evangelical Free Church National Board. Of course, he just happens to be sitting at the table next to ours as we were having a lunch break. Some other pastors were sitting at our table, and I was sharing the story of how the shelter started, the battles fought, and my sermon where I said, "I don't give a rat's behind if I stand alone with Jesus and turn off the lights on my way out if it is over."

The next thing I know, he is sitting at my table and asking if I preach like that behind the pulpit. Ron beat me to the punch and answered with a resounding, "Oh, yeah!" Dale's response was, "I love that!" That amazed me, but not as much as his next question. He informed me that he was getting speakers for the Evangelical Free Church's National Conference and then asked if I would be willing to go to San Diego, California, and repeat that story. You know how sometimes you have a knee-jerk reaction when you speak without thinking it through? That's just exactly what I did, so I said, "Yes." It took a while to sink in that I would be speaking to a crowd of men and women with master's degrees and doctorates, and as I later found out, professors at major seminaries. Jesus set it all up and the Holy Spirit shot the answer out of my mouth and somehow kept my mind on hold (which is more normal than not) and I said "yes". Well afterwards, while Ron and I were in our room that night, I looked at him and said, "What did I just do? This is nuts. I am not qualified to speak at a national conference. Are you kidding me? I speak using Maine hicks' slang; I hardly passed English in school, let alone speak it well." All of a sudden I had the "hog horrors" (slang for scared to death).

What did this "great man of faith and courage" do? I went home, sat on my bed again, raised my hands to heaven, and cried like a baby. In the midst of sobbing, I called my district superintendent, who was leaving for a trip out of the country, to ask him, "Why me?" Dr. Ves Sheely took my call and informed me he was on his way out with bags in hand, so this had to be very short, and knowing me as he did, he knew he needed to emphasize that point. So I said, "Yes, I need to know 'Why me?' You know who and what I am. I'm the last man in the country to go and speak at a national conference. I saw the brochure and you have famous and important speakers and I'm this dumb hick from Skowhegan. To make it worse, I was told I was to be an "inspirational speaker." He said, "I've got to go, but my quick answer is for you to read Acts 4:13." So, I stopped crying like a baby and went to get my Bible to look up this verse and see his one sentence answer to my overwhelming problem.

If you do not know Acts 4:13, here it is: "When they saw the courage of Peter and John and realized that they were unschooled, ordinary men, they were astonished and they took note that these men had been with Jesus." Wow! I get it. I stopped crying and looked upwards toward heaven and proclaimed, "Thanks, Jesus, for making it so clear to me! The dumber the man, the greater the glory goes to you. They will surely say it has to be God because this man is not smart enough or talented enough to accomplish all of this on his own." As wild as that may sound, it helped.

My wife and I arrived in San Diego and I called Ves to get some advice on what to wear. We conceived a plan for us to meet prior to me speaking that evening so he could hear what I was going to say and "smooth me out" if I was really bad with my slang. We had a good plan, but it wasn't the one that Jesus had for me. Ves told me to meet in the lobby that evening. I agreed and went to the lobby, but no Ves.

I asked around and no one had seen Ves. We waited and waited, but no Ves. I couldn't call him because my cell phone was back at the motel, charging. Finally, it's time for this part of the conference to begin. We go in and sit down at a table and here comes Ves. I asked where he had been and he said "I was in the lobby waiting for you." He asked where we had been and I said, "In the lobby waiting for you." Now how ridiculous does that sound? The answer was there were two lobbies and I did not know that he took it for granted I would go to the correct one. He never told me there were two. I guess he thought I was smart enough to figure that out. Wrong!

So we are now together and I am about to discuss this with him when someone comes over and whispers to him. He then turns to me and says, "They want you up there now, so I guess you are on your own." That's not what I wanted to hear, but once again, Jesus asks me to believe I can walk on water when all evidence says I'm in a world of mess. Ves stands up and begins to introduce me and while he's describing my ministry I'm thinking, "Is that me he's talking about?" I struggle even today with being introduced as a man of faith. I see myself as a man who had no choice! To me, that's different.

I walk up on stage and Ves hands me the mic. I look out over all the faces of men and women who are out of my league, and for a second which seemed more like an eternity, I froze. I was so afraid of how they would react, or simply not react, to a guy with my lack of credentials. The Holy Spirit must have opened my mouth, but what came out at first would never be confused with being inspired. All that came to my mind at the moment was the old comedy show The Beverly Hillbillies as they rode into Beverly Hills. So, I poetically stated, "The Beverly Hillbillies have just come to San Diego." What a dumb thing to say! But the Holy Spirit filled that place and people laughed and cheered. I relaxed and thought, "This is cool. I can do it!" Jesus took over and there were two standing ovations, clapping, and cheering. I thought I was in a high school pep rally. Jesus, once again, opened the Red Sea and let me cross!

Following the speech, many came to be prayed over to gain more faith, and many asked the same questions. "Would you come and share at my church," and "Are you going to write a book?" I saw the door opening at that moment and knew Jesus was going to use me to travel and speak. He showed me He had a message, and like Moses, all He needed was a willingness and He would offset the weaknesses. Moses had a speech impediment and I was like Larry the Cable Guy with a pulpit. I would not get over wondering how I would be accepted at churches that were used to pastors and speakers with degrees and a whole bunch of letters before and after their names. But I said, "Here we go Jesus. You open the doors and give me the words, and I'm willing to leave my comfort zone and go where there is an opening."

Because of the reception in San Diego, I returned home with a fresh spirit and vigor. I was now looking for Jesus to use this ministry to be a part of a revival in America. I now believed He was going to use the homeless as fuel for that revival. And as I began to travel throughout New England, I saw the impact it was having on believers. Also, checks began to come in from all over the country. I saw one from Washington State and read the letter that came with it. These folks were at the conference and were moved to give. Many letters with checks in them began to arrive. I saw light at the end of the tunnel.

CHAPTER 14

THE SHELTER WASN'T only affecting Christians, but also non-Christians as they were being moved to support us. All I could think of was when God used Gentiles to finance the rebuilding of the Jerusalem Temple following captivity.

Things were looking different at home as well. One day, a police officer dropped off a young man at the shelter. As the young man is entering my church, I walk over to the police cruiser. I had been getting used to the police putting me down whenever they would come near to me. They would always comment on how bad I was for taking in some of these men and allowing them to live in town. But I would always walk up to them and greet them in a friendly manner. To say I always "felt" friendly would be an outright lie. But little did I know that Jesus was working His plan to turn them around. As I approached the cruiser, I saw something that looked way out of place. The officer was smiling at me! I thought, "Don't toy with me like a cat playing with a mouse prior to the kill." He simply asked me a question: "Pastor Berry, do you know who that young man is right there?" I admitted I had no idea whatsoever. The young man was the Police Sergeant's son and he'd been kicked out of group homes, and nobody would take him, including his parents. If we didn't take him, he would've been out on the streets. From that moment on, the police department looked at us differently. They went from trying to shut me down to actually sponsoring my fundraising golf tournament. What a change in attitude!

Now Jesus was showing His power at home in Skowhegan and the effects of His power as I traveled to speak, taking a team of homeless with me. I remember speaking at one church and Jesus showed me how much impact this ministry was having. A lady came up to me while I was in the foyer meeting folks as they were leaving. She walked right up to me, not dressed any better than the folks in the shelter. She handed me a one dollar bill and then made me cry. She shared how she had come off the streets herself just two weeks ago. She then said "This is all the money I have and I want to give it to the homeless in your shelter." My first response was to beg her to keep it. I was really feeling bad. When she insisted, however, I accepted it and went home to tell the homeless. We all had a good cry while praising Jesus for touching this lady to give all she had. I had read and taught the story of the widow who gave the copper coins, the last two she possessed, where Jesus stated, "Truly I tell you, this poor widow has put in more than all the others. All these people gave their gifts out of their wealth; but she out of her poverty put in all she had to live on" (Luke 21:3-4). I have been so amazed to watch Scripture lived out before my eyes.

This homeless ministry has touched people in ways I never would have imagined. This moment left a lasting impression upon me, and many more were forthcoming.

I received a call from another area homeless shelter that operated differently than we did. During the daytime, all residents were made to leave in the morning and not return until evening. We operate on a 24/7 basis. I can't see putting people out on the same streets we were bringing them in from. The head of that shelter told me a story and asked me to help. It was one of the saddest I'd heard up until now. She told me a young lady had given birth to a baby, and her parents wouldn't allow her to stay with them. The father wanted no part of her or the baby. She came to their shelter and then had the baby. A problem occurred during the delivery and caused her to hemorrhage after delivery. She was told by the doctor to go home and keep her feet elevated to prevent further bleeding. Now the real problem set in. The lady that ran the shelter couldn't allow her to stay in the shelter during the daytime. She told me that unless I could take her she would walk the streets, bleeding and carrying a newborn baby. All of this was in the winter in Maine! I only had men at that time and could not take her. That was killing me! I sat in my office with hands raised to Jesus crying out, "Either help me start another shelter for women and children or don't let me receive any more phone calls like this one!" As soon as I prayed, God brought a church to mind. It was a small church with part of the building that had not been finished. It was located in Solon, a small town north of

Skowhegan. The pastor was an old friend, Tim Hunt. I called him and asked if he would meet me at Dunkin' Donuts for coffee and doughnuts. He agreed, and we met. I shared my story and told him I believed Jesus wanted his church to take in homeless women and children. I can't say he jumped up and down and cried out, "Praise the Lord!" He did say he'd talk to his leaders about taking it to the church. He also mentioned they were small and had no money, which was a major reason the building never got finished. I assured him that I would supply all the materials and send crews to work on it and some staff to run it. All I was asking for was the use of the building. He asked how I was planning on doing this, and this "great man of faith" looked him in the eyes and stated clearly, "I don't know." But, I quickly added, "I'm building one I can't afford and have no idea how we will do it, so why not build two?"

As I have already pointed out, I'm not that smart, but I knew one thing for sure. I could not field any more of these kinds of phone calls and do nothing about it. His church voted to allow us to use the building, and in a very few weeks we had residents. God so blessed this ministry and the New Hope Evangelical Free Church in Solon that within six months they took it over and have since built a new facility of their own. Jesus only needs us to give Him a chance to show His power and He will do it.

CHAPTER 15

THESE SORTS OF things inspired one of my messages that I preach when I travel. It's entitled the "Battle of the Daddies." The text is found in 1 Kings Chapter 18. Elijah challenges the 450 prophets of Baal. Israel was turned away from God and the altar was in ruins. Elijah tells all the prophets to call on Baal to take up an offering of a bull on a pile of wood. He tells them to go first and see what Baal can do. Then he will call on his God and show them what He can do. I call it the Battle of the Daddies, because in Romans 8:15, Paul says we can call God "Abba Father" or "Daddy." I now pray to "Dad" when in a tight spot. As a kid we used to say, "My daddy can whoop your daddy." Now that was never going to happen, but it fit this message very well. Elijah says, "Call on 'your daddy' and I will call on mine, and mine will whoop yours." Elijah was not afraid to put God to the test and let Him show off His glory to encourage His people to worship and honor Him. Elijah taunts the other prophets because the offering remains untouched on the pile of wood. It's truly funny how he eggs them on. Then he tells the ones preparing his offering to water it down in order to make it even more difficult. He leaves no question in the minds of the observers that he serves the one and only true God and Dad. God takes up the offering and the water around the offering that had filled the trenches. Israel then proclaimed, “The Lord—he is God! The Lord—he is God!”

That’s what I see God doing with this ministry. He’s pushing me to ask things of Him I would have NEVER asked any time in the past. I find myself pushed into a corner where I have no choice but to beg Him to do miracles. Don’t get me wrong. No way am I saying I am like Elijah or any other great man in the Bible. I know who and what I am. I’m simply a dumb hick from Skowhegan, Maine. But God is the same God who did all those miracles then, and I believe He wants to show His people that He can, and will, do them today.

At one point in the building of the men’s shelter, I experienced someone responding in a similar fashion as the Israelites who observed this miracle. A social worker, who had been coming since the very beginning, brought another social worker to show him the building. The two were standing in front of the building when the one shared something with the other. I heard him say, “I’m not religious. Never been to a church and never believed in God. But I know how this building is being built and I know this is a miracle, and so there must be a God.” I do not know if he ever accepted Jesus, as he was sent to work somewhere else, but what I do know is Jesus was glorified that day and that's the reason He's doing these miracles in America today as He did in Israel in the past.

In the midst of all the miracles, the building continues to grow. The donations of funds get stretched out a long way as companies and individuals donate materials at no cost. I have become America's biggest beggar and am not ashamed of it. I have never begged for a penny for myself or family, but I will for the homeless. I began contacting companies, both local and out of the state. I was amazed how God moved so many to do so much.

We needed plumbing, so I contacted a local plumber named Dan to see if he could donate the plumbing. He shared how business was slow due to the economy. He believed in what I was doing with the homeless and said he would donate his labor if some of the homeless would work with him, but there was no way could he donate all the pipes and other materials for the plumbing. We had some money so I agreed to pay for the materials as well as supply helpers. When the job was complete and we were going to pay him, Jesus touched his heart. He said, "I can't take your money. I will get by without it." God honored his generosity toward the homeless. All of a sudden, his business began to prosper to the point where he had to hire more crews and shared how he realized God blessed him for blessing us. God's power was evident to all who got involved.

Later on, when we needed to tile all the floors I approached Mike who owns a flooring store in Winslow, Maine. I asked if he could help, and he did way more than I expected. He contacted a distributor who donated all of the tile for the entire project. He then contacted other flooring contractors who donated their time to the project. Mike shares how he had one crew and was just barely able to keep them working because of the tight economy. But after he helped the homeless, his business exploded. He had to hire more crews and still could not keep up. He told me how a local school district needed some rooms done and contacted him. He said, “You won’t believe what happened next.” I told them I couldn’t even go to the building, measure it, and give a bid on the job. He said they kept insisting they wanted him and only him. He said what happened next could only be described as a “God thing.” The superintendent of the school said, “I don’t need a bid from you. Do it when you can and simply send me a bill.” That does not happen! But with this crazy ministry to the homeless, Jesus makes the impossible possible on a regular basis. God is showing off and getting the glory. You can see how we never had much money yet always had enough to get by daily and keep the project moving so we could maintain “progress” that would appease the State Fire Marshall and allow us to continue.

CHAPTER 16

I AM BEGINNING to understand how the Israelites had to live in the desert with manna falling daily from heaven. They were only to pick up what was needed per person or family each day. The story is told in Exodus 16:14-24. Moses commanded them not to gather more than needed, and when they did, it rotted and was full of maggots so it was a useless endeavor. Jesus is teaching me not to worry about tomorrow, but to simply trust He will supply the needs today. Now I am not saying He works this way with every church. When I shared this with one pastor, he quickly told me that often churches need to have more than enough for today so they have something to share with us. I accept that, and pray many churches will be blessed to the point they can share with us to care for the homeless.

I truly believe the poor in America are the responsibility of Christ's Church and not the government. At last count, thirty plus cities developed an ordinance that makes it illegal to feed the homeless. Are you kidding me? But having said that, look at the opportunity Jesus is laying before the church to begin a harvest that would rival the

"Great Awakenings" of church history. Our tiny little church ministry is seeing over 300 salvations per year as we feed, clothe, and house the homeless. Wearing a bracelet with the inscription "What would Jesus do, WWJD" is great, but the churches in America need to step up to the plate and begin to show America just exactly what Jesus would do. You know what's truly sad? In Matthew 9:37-38, Jesus says, "The harvest is plentiful but the workers are few. Ask the Lord of the harvest, therefore, to send out workers into His harvest field." We are standing in the middle of the field and simply looking at the harvest that's really ripe while failing to respond. We pray for revival in America, and it is staring us right in the face! As I travel and speak, one statement continues to resound: We want to see Jesus do miracles like He's doing in Skowhegan, but the reason He's doing miracles is simply because miracles are needed to obey His command to care for the poor. If you have no desire to join the harvest, then you have no need for miracles.

In Galatians 2:8-10, Paul shares how the Jerusalem Council recognized his gift and calling to carry the gospel to the Gentiles. He states in verse 10, "All they asked was that we should continue to remember the poor, the very thing I was eager to do." While America is turning her back on the homeless, God is calling out for His people to seize the opportunities of showing his love and compassion. As I travel, I see God's people weep because of the stories. Now we must not simply weep, but reach out and show America what Jesus can do when His body is filled with the Holy Spirit and moved with compassion.

Can you imagine what the face of the church of America would look like if the news began carrying stories of how the cities no longer have a homeless problem because the Church of Christ has arisen and taken care of them? This country's nuisance is the church's opportunity.

CHAPTER 17

MY HEART LEAPS in my chest as I recall some of the miracles I've seen with the homeless. One homeless man, named Butch, came to know Jesus. A very short time later, a physical problem surfaced. He shared with us how he could not swallow. He went to the hospital and they ran tests on his throat. The reason he could not swallow was he had a growth developed in his esophagus. They did a biopsy and found it to be a malignant, cancerous tumor. He was scared to death. He hadn't been saved very long, so he didn't grasp what God could do if He so desired. He heard the stories of all the other miracles that had taken place, so he asked me to pray for him to have a miracle. A group of us gathered around him, I anointed him with oil, and we all prayed for a healing miracle. I know God does not heal everyone, but I know He can. The next morning prior to him going in for surgery, he said, "Pastor, I can swallow!" I wasn't sure it meant anything, but he was encouraged. He went in for pre-surgical x-rays and they told him they had no explanation, but the tumor was no longer there. I had a great explanation. I wish I could have shown the entire world this man's response to being healed. He cried, and cried some more. He kept asking, "Why would God do that for me?" He couldn't speak of it without crying. As great as that was, imagine this: What if we left him on the street? Maybe God would've healed him anyway, but we wouldn't have had the privilege of seeing it, and God would not have received the glory, because we wouldn't have known Butch.

None of this would've been possible unless God moved others to join us in raising up this building. I remember when Ronnie and I were at a conference at Camp Spofford, and a lady overheard us talking. She came and sat down and wanted to know all about it. She told us she was a member of the Evangelical Free Church in Windsor Locks, Connecticut. She then got up and found her pastor and had him come and listen to our story. They both shared how they wanted the church to be "hands on" with a missions project. They said this was exactly what they were looking for at this time. Of course it was!

They not only sent a team to work on the building, but purchased and brought the materials needed for it. I was blown away as they showed up with carpenters, electricians, locksmiths, and laborers. The pastor had my kind of skills, so he was relegated to picking up nails that had fallen on the ground. Everyone had a good laugh over that, and the jokes poured out like a river flowing over a dam.

It became obvious that God was going to supply all we needed, despite the bad economy. He was teaching me things I surely never learned in Bible school. For instance, one day the man in charge of doing the welding, Jon, came to me and said, "It's time to build the metal fire escape." I replied, "Fine." He, however, told me that it was not fine at all. He needed another welder to work on the project, and it needed to be a certified welder, not simply a common laborer. The homeless were not going to fill the bill on this one. It was in the afternoon and he needed one by the next morning in order to continue to "show progress." I asked how much it would cost to hire a certified welder. He informed me it would be $50 per hour and the job would last approximately three weeks. I'm no mathematician, but I could figure out that the math on this one did not add up, as there was no money at the present time. So I threw my hands into the air and prayed, "Dad, I need a welder!" I began to sound like a child bugging his parents for something constantly. The difference is He never seemed to get exasperated by my constant begging. He simply continued to give me what I asked for whenever the needs arose. This was a perfect illustration of that fact.

I was traveling that evening and as I came through Norridgewock, the next town over and my hometown, I saw a hitchhiker. It was a cold day and he was way underdressed for this Maine weather. I pulled over and asked where he was going. He said, "I just got out of jail and do not have anywhere to go. I'm looking for some food and even shelter. Do you know of such a place?" I said, "I do. As it so happens, I run a homeless shelter. Would you like to come with me?" He jumped in and we headed for some warmer clothes, hot food, and a warm place to sleep. I then asked him, "What's your name and what do you do when you are not in jail or hitchhiking?" He said, "My name is Ernie, and I am a certified welder." I replied, "Of course you are!"

Ernie had worked on major projects all over the U.S. He was one of the finest welders in the country but was an alcoholic. That landed him in jail and off the jobs. He informed me he would stay with me until the job was complete. He did two things: First, he turned down $50 an hour jobs, and second, he stayed clean right up until he left. He left the day the stairs were completed. He added a special touch to the job. He made three crosses that stand out loud and clear to the glory of God. I continue to praise Jesus for the opportunities to see these things done today and realize what I would have missed if I simply looked the other way and left a homeless man standing in the cold. The government may say, "Don't feed them," but Jesus says, "Look how I bless you when you do!"

CHAPTER 18

IT SEEMS AS though God has gone out of His way to show us that it is "in God we trust," like it says on our money, and He can do that many times without using money. A couple of situations that came not far apart sure drove this point home.

One day, Dr. Don Dubois visited me at my office and offered to start a free medical clinic to care for the homeless. At that time, we had a room which had been used as a nursery. I showed it to him and he said it would work just fine. We would actually make two small rooms out of that one large one. One room would be used for triage and the other for examinations. I told him I had no money to remodel the rooms as medical rooms. He said, "No problem. I will finance the needed work on the rooms and get the hospital in town to donate the examining table, as well as some other materials to get it up and running." Once again, I stood back and shook my head at the idea; we now had our own free clinic within the church building. He started working alone, but others began to volunteer their time as well. We had enough doctors and nurses to run it and be open one day a week.

I still had a tough time comprehending the fact we have this to offer the homeless. This "no budget" operation that lives by daily checking the mail to see if we keep the lights on and pay the mortgage has more to offer the homeless then the shelter with budgets and money. Many come with no insurance, or even state help, so to be able to offer them such services goes beyond anything or any words that can be described on paper in a book. I wish everyone could see some of their faces when we announce the doctor will be in today and you don't have to pay a penny!

One day I got a call and the man said, "My name is Jeff. I heard you speak at my church and would like to come and speak with you." Jeff showed up and made a statement that caught me off guard. He said, "I own a farm just around the corner from you. I used to have a business there, but I sold my business and the farm is sitting there vacant. He went on to explain that while I was speaking at his church about this homeless ministry, he believed Jesus was telling him to give me the farm to use to grow food, raise animals, etc. to aid in feeding the homeless. He asked if I could go with him to look at it and see if it was something I could use. I have to admit I was a little skeptical and figured it was an old farm that would rival that of the comedy movie Ma and Pa Kettle. I was really underestimating Jesus Christ. It was a beautiful farm with a newly renovated house and beautiful barns. He went on to explain there was a new tractor at my disposal, as well. Of course, there was! Note he didn't say the house was to be occupied, simply the fields and barns for raising crops and housing animals. But something was going on at that time that I was unaware of until later. A couple was praying for God's help with their housing situation. Derek had been my first chief of staff at the shelter. He had gotten married and moved on. His wife had some children and desired to take in foster children. The home they had was more than they could now afford because of job situations. They were on the verge of being homeless for the first time. I was totally unaware of any of this going on. But all of a sudden, I asked Jeff if I could put a family in the house to oversee the property, because there would be a need to watch out for the building and oversee the care of crops and animals. I did not feel comfortable simply sending crews in the daytime; I would feel more comfortable having a caretaker there all the time. He asked if I had someone in mind, and guess whose name came to me at that moment. Derek, of course! He reached into his pocket and handed me the keys to the farm. I called Derek and he shared how they were praying and this farm was the answer to their prayers. Only Jesus can orchestrate something like this!

We had begun to get food from a local market, but the needs were growing and now it looked like we could supplement it with the farm. I shared all this with Ronnie and my treasurer, Norton. Ronnie is seeing this like me, a gift from God that's meeting needs (i.e., Derek's family) before we even got started. Norton saw it differently, from a treasurer's perspective. He said, "I'm not sure we should do this as we have no money to plow the land, no money to fertilize it after it's plowed, and no money for seeds if we fertilize it." A very logical argument, I have to admit. But I turned to him and said, "Look at all God has given us, and we had no money then. Don't you think we can trust Him for fertilizer?" Actually, I literally said "manure" because that's a main fertilizer in Maine. At that, we both laughed and went ahead with the project, looking to see how Jesus would once again orchestrate what was humanly impossible.

The next morning before we prayed, I brought up the need for someone to plow the fields and supply fertilizer at no cost to us. I barely got it out of my mouth when a new resident stood up and asked if I knew who he was. I didn't, as new people were beginning to show up almost daily and I hadn't had time to sit down with this man to hear his story. He said, "They call me 'Goody' and my family are all farmers. My relatives are also mostly farmers. I heard your story last night and made some phone calls. The fields will be plowed and fertilized at no cost to the shelter." I said, "Of course, they will!"

That morning was the beginning of what would once again blow my mind. Jeff called and informed me that a local seed company would supply all the seed we could use. We simply had to make a list and pick them up. Of course they would! The next day I got a call from a family in town that owned greenhouses and sold plants. They said they saw me on TV and heard my story. They wanted to donate some plants for the garden. Of course, they did! I showed up at their residence with my pickup and they started to laugh. I could not, for the life of me, figure out what was so funny. Then they asked me, “Do you know how many plants we are donating?” I admitted I was ignorant of the situation, which is not always that uncommon with me. They led me to a huge greenhouse, and it had a large stack of plants in front of it. I’m thinking maybe I would have to make another trip, but I do not see why it is so hilarious. I said, “Thanks for these plants. I will be back to get what I can’t take on the first trip.” Then they informed me that those were not all the plants. They gave me the entire greenhouse! There were so many that we gave many of them away because we did not have enough area to plant them all. I am thinking, “Are you kidding me, Jesus?” Talk about your manna from heaven! But, Jesus had more for me.

I got another call later that day from another seed company. The man on the phone said he saw me on TV and his company wanted to supply potatoes for seed, and some were also still edible. So this time I took my pickup truck and my trailer along. I was ready for what Jesus had in store for me this time. The manager took me into this massive warehouse full of potatoes. I asked him, “Which ones are for the shelter?” He said, “You can have all of them if you want them.” Of course, I could! I thanked him and loaded my truck and trailer and explained that’s all I could use at the time as there were too many to plant or eat. They would simply end up spoiling and I could not see doing that. Now take special note: all without spending one dollar! Can Jesus give us a farm and supply it all without money? You betcha! Of course, he can!

CHAPTER 19

IT HAS BEEN a never-ending list of things that continued to amaze me. One of them being how Jesus showed me the face of homelessness wasn't always as I pictured it, or as others seem to want to portray it.

One day I was standing in the parking lot of the shelter, and this fancy car drove in. It got my attention in a hurry, as I was not accustomed to seeing cars like this at the shelter. The car stopped and a man and a woman, both dressed to the nines, stepped out. The lady approached me and asked if this was the homeless shelter. I said, "Yes." She started to cry and shared how she needed to find a shelter for her brother as he could no longer live with her and her husband. She said he was an alcoholic and had spent last night on a park bench. I asked when he would be arriving and she said, "That's him with me." I was shocked to put it mildly. He was dressed better than me, clean cut, and a good looking guy. I thought, "Are you kidding me? This has got to be a joke!" I looked more like a homeless man than he did. I walked over to him, shook his hand, and introduced myself. I asked his name and the answer blew me away more than his appearance. He said, "I'm Mark LaVerdiere." Now, if you are not from around here, that name may not mean anything. But in Central Maine, that's like saying "Kennedy" in Massachusetts. My first thought was there must be some other LaVerdieres. Wrong! His dad was the well-known editor and columnist for the local paper and his brother is a judge in one county. Not a name in line with homelessness! But he was, and the reason he was dressed so well is because his huge wardrobe was all he had left. He went from the penthouse to the outhouse over a three-year period. He went through two divorces and the last one did him in. He sold off lands he owned to pay his lawyer and turned to alcohol. He ended up selling his boats and cars to purchase the alcohol. Because of the drinking, he lost his job with a major paper mill where he had been earning more than $100,000 per year. His drinking got him on the outs with his family, so no help there, and he could no longer stay with them because they didn't want a drunk around. He finally got so low he attempted suicide. He carries the scars on his throat to this day. He tells how he heard them pronounce him dead during surgery and then heard them say he had a pulse. So now his sister brought him to the shelter.

Everyone does a chore, and his first day here he was assigned a mop to wash hallways. Usually, residents are at the shelter for some time before I offer them a staff position. But I was in need of an office administrator and he was just what the doctor ordered. He worked in management in the past, so I asked if he would like to trade that mop for a computer and set of staff keys. He said he would and down the road he became my new chief of staff. I could never have afforded an administrator with his credentials. But God gives me what I need without giving me money. Mark has since gotten married to a lady who came to the shelter off the street with two children. That took place at a period of time later when the men's shelter was completed. He is one of the members of my homeless teams that travels to present the ministry and to share the miracles. One day, maybe he'll speak at your church or organization, and believe me when I say you will be blown away and blessed! He was definitely the exception to the rule. Every once in a while a story similar to Mark's would appear, but I have to admit not many.

On the other end of the spectrum, I had a man call me and ask if we had openings for a man. I assured him we did and he brought him over later that morning. Boy, was it cold that day. The night before, it was below zero; Not a night to be homeless. The man arrived with this very short little man. He had a beard and long hair. He was not dressed like Mark. His clothes looked like he'd slept in them for quite a while. He went by the nickname Spike. He wouldn't speak and simply stood with his head down. So I asked the man who brought him, "What's his story?" He replied, "He's been seen on the streets for quite some time. I do not know him personally. I came out of my house this morning and he was curled up in the fetal position under my breezeway." The breezeway only had a roof and no sides or ends. It was wide open, but obviously the best shelter he could find that night. His beard and hair were full of frost and ice. He had sores on his feet, and we learned later that he had untreated diabetes. Over time he became a part of the shelter, like the furniture. He was just there. He started to speak in time and told his stories of living on the streets. He was a favorite of many of us, especially my wife. He came to love and be loved by everyone. He later got gangrene in the legs but refused to have them amputated. He went to be with Jesus. His life was expanded because we took him in. Ours was enriched by the experience of knowing him. When I travel and speak, I show a DVD with Spike's face on it. He will always be a part of the shelter and now is truly "sheltered by Jesus."

CHAPTER 20

As the numbers grew, the blessings continued to flow. One area that was growing was the laundry needs. We started out with one old used washer and one old used dryer. When you have no budget, you make do and we did just that. Early on, each person was responsible for their own laundry. But Jesus moved again and the owner of an appliance store in Enfield, Connecticut donated new washers and dryers for the shelter. Carl is one of the members of Windsor Locks Congregational Evangelical Free Church that sent crews to build the new shelter. So now with the new washers and dryers, we began to offer laundry service for the residents. I put a staff member in charge and he would see to it that each resident had their clothes washed, dried, and sent back to them. Some ladies made laundry bags, so each one would leave a bag of dirty laundry and pick up their bag filled with clean laundry. It continues to amaze me how Jesus continued to grow us to this point. We now offered a warm bed, hot food, clean laundry, and medical care. I catch myself standing back and looking at all of this in a state of awe with the thought, "What's next, Jesus?"

This ministry has put me in touch with some incredible people who respond with things I would never have thought of asking Jesus to provide. One such individual is Jeff. He has truly astounded me with his love and generosity for the homeless. I met him when I spoke in Wethersfield, Connecticut, a truly awesome group of believers with hearts for the homeless. Jeff approached me at the end of my message to share his story with me. He shared how he had a commercial landscaping business. He was very successful at this time, but was at one time only about a day from being homeless himself. He explained how he wanted to do something for the homeless. He decided to landscape around our church and new men's shelter. He brought his crew and all the materials from Connecticut. I was shocked someone would do this.

Later on, I spoke at his church again and shared a story that moved his heart to do something truly amazing. I had a large group to be baptized and had contacted a local church concerning the use of their baptismal. They agreed and I set the date. But then I received a call from their church secretary. She asked if the rumor was true that we were battling a bed bug problem at the time. I said that it was true. We were getting it under control, but like many places in the country dealing with large numbers of people, bed bugs were appearing. So I was asked not to hold the baptism there as some people were concerned we might carry a bed bug into their church. I told my staff to find something in which we could put water in order to have the baptism go forward. I got a call from one of them and he said he found something with dimensions that would accommodate the baptism. The container was 8' x 2' x 2'. I said, "Perfect. Great job!" They went on to explain the container was at Tractor Supply and it was a horse water trough! I said, "Boys, does that fit!" We baptized 16 in that new baptismal! Jeff heard the story and said, "I will come to Skowhegan and build you a great baptismal." And did he ever! He built a huge one out in our park behind the shelter. It is made of stone with a stone deck all around it. He had a crew work for three weeks building and landscaping around it. I was told if we had the work done it would cost about $30,000. It is gorgeous. I have a picture of it on my DVD I show when traveling and speaking. We baptized 26 new believers in it the first time we used it. I was truly blessed to also have the honor of baptizing Jeff with the homeless. He had been saved and baptized previously, but wanted to identify not only with Jesus but also with the homeless, bed bugs and all!

Jesus has truly blessed me to have all these awesome people in my life, both the homeless, and those with a heart for the homeless. Wow, I could have missed out on all of this if I chose not to take in that first homeless man. I pray more pastors and churches will seek these blessings as we are privileged to serve Jesus in America.

CHAPTER 21

ONE DAY I had an amazing and puzzling visitor. He came in a van with Michigan plates on it. I figured he was living around here somewhere and simply disregarded the plates. I asked him his name and he told me "Joseph." I asked him his full name and he said, "Simply Joseph." I asked how long he'd been homeless and he replied, "I'm not homeless, nor have I ever been homeless." Now he had me curious, so I asked if he stopped by for some food. He replied that his van was full of food; it was fully equipped for him to live in it. I asked, "Are you visiting friends or relatives?" He replied, "No, I do not know a soul in Maine. Never been here before." So I asked, "Are you on vacation?" He answered, "No." I said, "Joseph, I'm really confused. Why are you here in Maine and especially at a homeless shelter?" What he shared next astounded me. He said, "God showed me a vision of this church with the Holy Spirit enveloping it. I asked God what it was all about and he told me to go to Skowhegan, Maine, and encourage Pastor Berry. God sent me here for you."

Now, I do not know where you may stand on such things, but my first thought was, "This man has run into some really bad pizza!" He confounded me even more as I saw him speak to one of my residents. We called him "Carnie," a nickname he picked up traveling and working with carnivals. His speech was so incoherent we couldn't understand him. Joseph laid hands on him and prayed, and immediately his speech cleared up and remained clear to this day. Joseph was gone the next morning and I have had no contact with him since. This ministry continues to stun me with the miracles that continually happen. I never believed these things happen today, and if I was reading this I wouldn't believe it myself. But since I saw it and heard it, all I can do is share it.

CHAPTER 22

I AM ALWAYS amazed at the talent level of people that wind up at the shelter and at their hearts that desire to help and give back. One day I received a call from a local nursing home. They said, "We heard you help people in the community and we have no other place left to turn for help. The lady on the phone began to share a story that killed my heart. She shared how they had a man at the nursing home that, due to the effects of diabetes, was now confined to a wheelchair. Now that was not mind blowing as many people are in the same condition. The difference was his wife was unable to take him home because they had no handicap ramp. His wife had tried to get help on local and state levels. She was told there was no funding due to the economic conditions. So this poor man was in a position of being unable to go home with no answer in sight. The wife shared how they had run a food pantry out of their home for years, but with poor health conditions they were forced to close. Now they needed help and no one came to their aid. I contacted local businesses to ask if they would donate money for me to purchase materials for the ramp. The lumber yard sold me the materials at cost. After I purchased the materials, a team of homeless carpenters built the ramp. What an awesome day when I saw this man enter his home because a group of homeless men made it possible. "Those kind of people" looked pretty good to that couple on that day! Again, had we never taken in the homeless, I would never have been able to share in this experience.

We were now getting prepared for our grand opening of the men's shelter. It continues to amaze me that God supplied all the funds, materials, and manpower to complete this project. The day we had our celebration, the same chief of police that attempted to shut me down was present to cut the ribbon. In his speech, as he cut it, he proclaimed that he had changed his mind about me and the shelter. He said, "I saw Pastor Berry and this shelter as the worst thing to ever happen to Skowhegan, Maine. I want to declare today, this is one of the best things to come here." Jesus made my enemy my friend and took away a battle and replaced it with peace. I totally agree with the social worker who looked at the building and proclaimed, "This is a miracle; therefore, there is a God!" To me, the even greater miracle than the building was the change in the Chief. Maybe man could build a building, but only God can change a heart.

What a feeling of relief, satisfaction, joy, etc. I am praising God and feeling like a young colt just released from the barn in springtime. Not bad for a man in his mid-sixties! But, Jesus had more coming my way that I did not foresee.

CHAPTER 23

ONE DAY AS I sat in my office, a man came in and asked, "Are you Pastor Berry?" I said, "I am. Can I help you?" He replied, "I am told you do not turn anyone away. Is that true?" I assured him it was true. He said, "So you have available space today?" I replied that we did. He asked, "What do I need to do to enter the shelter?" I told him to go into the office and fill out a contract. He then added, "I need to go to my car and get my wife and three children." I said, "Wait a minute. You do know this is a men's shelter, don't you? Our shelter facility is all men, no women and no children." What he said next changed how I was about to do business. He told me he'd been to all the other shelters and none kept the families together. Either they accepted men or women and children, not families. Now this is in the middle of winter and he told me he had enough gas in his car to get him here and no more. He also stated, "I'd rather sit with my family in my car in your parking lot, and we all freeze to death instead of being separated. I will not walk away from my wife and children. We are homeless and all we have is each other."

Okay, so what do you say to that? Jesus backed me into a corner, again, and left me without a choice, again. I called my staff in and said, “Get some beds and put them back in the church. We are taking care of this family.” I had people immediately inform me, “You can’t do that!” Some reminded me how I was given time to build the men’s shelter and then move the men out of the church when it was finished. “You promised the fire marshals you wouldn’t have anyone living here once the shelter was completed.” I quickly responded with, “I did not promise that at all. I asked what I needed to do to keep them from shutting me down and tossing the homeless back onto the streets. They said build a new shelter, and as long as I showed progress, they’d leave me alone. I never once promised to never put anyone back in the church.” So a new chapter in the story of the homeless shelter is being written. I simply raised my hands toward heaven and said, “Okay, Jesus. This is yours, so here we go again.”

I often get asked, “Why?” The Holy Spirit brought a time in my life to mind that was very similar. One night when I was seven years old, in the dead of winter with a wind child of -40 degrees outside, our home burned down. It was just before Christmas, and we lost everything. We literally escaped with the clothes on our backs. I ran out with pajamas on and nothing on my feet. We lost our house, our barn with horses, our pets, Christmas tree, and all of our presents. My feet froze and the skin would peel off them over the next couple of years. That was so traumatic for a little boy. But I remembered clearly what I still had left to me. I had both Mom and Dad. They said, "Rick, it's going to be alright, Son." I believed them and the fears left.

As that dad stood there telling me his story, that's what flowed through my mind. Jesus took away any excuses and choices that I might have used. I had no choice but to take them in that day. I vividly remember the response of one lady when I finished sharing his story. She said, "I love your stories, but have to strongly disagree with one thing you said. You had a choice. Praise God you took that family in, but you did have a choice." Now I grasp what she was saying, but in my mind I had no choice. At least I had no choice I could live with later. How can I cry out to Jesus to keep doing His miracles and then send a family out in the cold? How could I live with myself if I turned this family away?

So the next chapter begins! As soon as word got out that a family was living in my church, my phone began to ring off the hook. I got calls from Social Services, Department of Human Services dealing with families, etc. It seemed like before I could blink, my church was full of bunk beds in rooms, including what used to serve as a library. There were even mattresses in my office and the sanctuary at night. The school bus began stopping at the church's front door and was leaving half full of children. We had 23 children at one point. As I said, God looked all over America for the dumbest man He could find and He picked me.

With the new challenges of having families—some with babies—came great joy and blessings. For example, ask yourself how you would feel having an eight-year old boy hug your leg and say, "Thanks for my bed!" I don't care if you are tougher than nails. When that little guy stares up at you with tears in his eyes and utters those words, you would melt like Frosty the Snowman in summertime. You have to understand what his bed is like. It's not like the ones you see in a furniture store that make your child cry out, "Daddy, I want one of those!" Oh no, not even close! My staff built the bunk beds out of rough lumber with a piece of plywood attached to 2x6's. You would find some that are more attractive in a hunting camp. But for a little boy who had been living in a car, it was magnificent! So now, how does that grab you?

CHAPTER 24

WE HAD A highly decorated veteran stay with us. He literally had a shoe box full of medals for serving our country. He went through a divorce and his wife got everything, but she didn't want the children. So Roger finds himself out on the street with his son and daughter. The Department of Human Services took his children and put them into foster homes. He came to the shelter and poured out his heart to me. He asked at our morning prayer time to pray God would reunite him with his children. He had a court date to go before a judge to request his children. The judge and Department of Human Services said, "If you are with Pastor Berry at the shelter and can take them there with you, we will give your children back to you." You talk about a man crying! He stayed at the shelter until he got his own home, and today has his children with him.

I remember on one precious day a lady came to check out the shelter. She was considering supporting us in some manner. She asked if she could see one of the families and speak to a child. We went to Roger's room. She saw his little boy and asked him this single question:

"Do you like it here?" He looked her right in the eye and never blinked. He said, "Of course I do!" She asked him why. He replied, "Because I have all I need. I have my dad and my sister, and we have a bed and food every day. I have all I need." That woman took to crying and couldn't say anything in response. I wanted to scream out, "Ask me again why I go through all of this for the homeless!" These families, with these precious little children have changed how we "do church." How many churches do you see where children help take up offering or hand out communion? Prior to the shelter being in the church, you had to be dressed "properly" (suit and tie) to do these things. And you haven't heard anything like a child pray over the offering before it is passed. These are things I never would have experienced if I refused to take in that first family. This ministry can give you the highest highs and send you to the lowest lows (as battles rage), but I couldn't picture ministry any other way today.

CHAPTER 25

It seemed like things were finally coming together and smoothing out for a while. I should know better by now. My wife and I were traveling when I got a phone call from Ronnie. He said, "Uncle Rick, I have some bad news." Not a great lead in for having a really great day. He went on to tell me that our chief supplier of food was going to stop giving to any groups that were not connected with the area food bank. Now we had applied to become members three times in the past and always with the same results. They turned us down because we made residents attend church, which was the same as the United Way's policy. They receive federal support so they have some regulations. We did not comply with all of them, and now the major food chains were going through them because of tax breaks. The IRS wanted a more accurate account of the amount of goods being donated. The food bank would be in charge of keeping the records for all donations which worked out better for the stores.

I understand where they were coming from and did not blame them. They had been so generous to us that there was no way I could complain. But when Ronnie shared all of this with me, my response was (and I can hardly believe it today), "Praise the Lord. Jesus must have something great on the way!" I said, "Could you get me the contact information for the food bank and I will go and see them personally." I was not involved with applying the three times we were turned down. Two other men completed the application, not me. The next morning, I grabbed Ted, who was on my staff at the time, and said, "Get in the truck. We're going to apply at the area food bank." On the way, I called my treasurer to let him know I was going. He reminded me that we'd been turned down three times and there was no sense in wasting my time and the shelter's gas money on this trip. But I told him I believed Jesus was behind this. It was on my heart and mind, so I would continue on my way. Little did I know that I was about to see Jesus work some miracles before this trip came to an end.

I set my GPS with the location of the office. As I've traveled all over the country, it has always landed me at the exact location for which I was headed. But something strange happened on this trip. It couldn't locate the correct destination. It took me to a place with only trees and no office and proclaimed in its normal way, "You have now reached your destination." So I thought I must've made a mistake in the address I had programmed. I checked, and it was exactly the correct location that I had programmed it to find. I turned around and started down the road when it says "Turn around at your next opportunity." I did and headed back the way I came and it told me again, "You have now reached your destination." This went on for about 20 minutes and I started to speak to it in a loud, pastoral manner (okay, maybe not all that pastoral). I told Ted to shut that thing off and we'd just turn around and drive to see if I could locate the place. I became truly upset as I continued on about 150 yards beyond the place I had been turning around, per request of my lovely GPS, and there it was! All I could say was, "Are you kidding me?"

I drove up to the building and Ted and I entered and stepped on an elevator to the second floor where the office was housed. I got off the elevator and walked up to the front desk to speak to the lady standing behind it. I began to share my story with this lady, who listened very sweetly and then informed me that, "This is just before Christmas and everyone but me is on vacation. I'm simply here to answer the phones and do some paperwork." She was simply a secretary. She did add that they are not taking on any more organizations and that we were at the wrong location. The Brewer warehouse services our area, so we would need to speak to them. She also added sweetly, "Would you like an application?"

I took the application, turned towards the elevator, and raised my hands in the air and cried out, "Dad, this is not what I expected! I expected you to do a miracle, and now I may have to explain to homeless people why I can't feed them any longer. There will be 23 hungry kids and about 70 hungry adults, and 400 families not able to get food from the pantry!" At that moment, the door to the elevator opened and out walked a man surrounded by a group of people. He walked right up to me and for what seemed like two lifetimes, we stared at each other. Finally, I had to ask him, "Should I know you?" He said, "I'm U.S. Congressman Mike Michaud." What happened next, Ted couldn't believe (and if I had stopped and thought for half a second I wouldn't have done it), but I grabbed him around the neck in sort of a head lock, poked my finger in his chest, and said, "You're just the man I'm looking for today!" Ted's mouth dropped and his eyes bugged out of his head. He was astounded that I grabbed a congressman. I said, "I'm Pastor Richard Berry, and I operate a homeless shelter in Skowhegan, Maine." I shared the story of the little boy hugging my leg and thanking me for his bed. I said, "If these folks turn me down, I can still give him a bed but he will go to bed hungry. Sir, can I toss your name around here?" He said, "Yes, you can."

For a moment, I now realized why my GPS was keeping me from getting here. Jesus took control of it and didn't allow me to arrive earlier, or I would have missed the congressman and his entourage altogether. While I was complaining about the food bank turning me down, I was standing in the middle of an open Red Sea and could not see it. But miracle number two was on the way. A lady, who was walking in front of the congressman was now standing in back of me. So from behind me I hear, "That will never happen. You will not get cut off. You will get more food than ever. We need more people like you and we will adjust our rules to fit you! Call this person in Brewer and tell her to give you a contract and tell her if there is a problem, she should call me." She never told me her name or who she was, but I heard the congressman call her Chrissy. She was a tiny blonde, standing five foot nothing and all I could think was, "Who is this person?" But I did as she said and when I was back in my pickup heading for home, I made the call. The lady in Brewer answered and I shared my story of how I needed a contract and if I didn't get one the food supply was going to come to an end. She was polite and said, "I can sympathize, but we have two problems. #1 we are not taking on new customers, and #2 it's almost Christmas and I was just leaving my office to begin a two-week vacation." So I replied, "I was just in Auburn and a lady that was with Congressman Michaud said if there was a problem to have you call her because she tells me I can have a contract." She then asked me to describe this lady. I described her as tiny and blond. She then asked if the congressman called her Chrissy, and I said, "Yes." All of a sudden she nearly blasts me off the phone, because she became so loud. She said, "We have no problem! You will not get cut off and as soon as I return from vacation, we will give you two contracts, one for a food kitchen and one for a food pantry." She went on to say, "You do not start at the bottom, do you? That little lady just happens to be the president of the food bank!" I replied, "Of course she is!"

Because of this meeting, we now receive food from three major stores, not just one. We started to get meat, along with vegetables, fruit, desserts, and bread. They filled our freezers to the point we had to get more freezers. The pantry was full, and people were leaving with smiles on their faces, knowing they would have full bellies as they go to bed at night. What looked like a problem ended up as a means for Jesus to send more manna from heaven to meet the growing numbers with great needs.

CHAPTER 26

In the midst of all this, God continues to work on changing lives. A very special case was a young man whose parents had been supporting the shelter for quite some time. They called and asked if I could take their son. They are a fantastic family that truly loves their son, but he got into drugs and became violent to the point they were afraid to have him living in their home with his younger siblings. He also battled a major temper that would flare up and he'd want to fight. He got disciplined a couple of times because of his actions at the shelter, but he kept coming back even after I put him out for disciplinary actions, or he'd find some people to take him in for a while.

One day he came to me and said he had decided to go into the Marines. He enlisted and was accepted. He almost failed to go, because he lost his temper and got into a fight at the shelter with one of the staff members. His recruiting sergeant was told of his actions, and he sat him down and laid out clearly how he was to act if he wanted to go into the Marines. That hit him hard. He was told that a man of honor does not get into petty fights because he cannot control his temper. He told me he was tired of his life, the way it had been, and wanted to truly change. He had been saved at a young age, but said he needed to get serious with God now. He began reading his Bible all the time and did make it into the Marines. He became a squad leader and was proud of how his life had changed. He gave the credit to Jesus. His first leave came and he wanted to go home to be with his family. They were skeptical, but said he could. They were blown away by what they saw and heard from their son when he arrived. He was told the bedrooms were filled with his siblings. He said, "Dad, I will gladly sleep in the cellar, because I do not deserve a bedroom after all the hurt I caused the family." His mom and dad hugged him and called me to say, "We have our son back! Thank you for having the shelter, because without that, we believe our son would be in jail or dead. Instead, we have a son again and are so proud of him."

I hope one day, when he leaves the Marines, to have him travel with my team and share his testimony to encourage other families not to give up hope. Jesus is still in the miracle business, and His greatest miracles are changed lives. Again, I would have missed the honor of seeing all of this if I chose not to take in the homeless. I still believe, with all my heart, I had no choice.

I remember one very unusual case that came on Christmas Eve. As I was growing up, my parents always made Christmas extra special. It was the best family time of the year. I remain a Christmas junkie to this day, with memories flowing in my head. But one Christmas Eve, as I was preparing for the Christmas Eve service at church, a lady and a young man, 18 years of age, came to my office. It turned out the lady was the boy's grandmother. She asked if I was Pastor Berry, and I said, "Yes." She said "You are the one they call 'The Miracle Man,' because of how lives change at this shelter." I quickly corrected her by saying, "No, ma'am. I work for The Miracle Man, Jesus Christ. The Holy Spirit changes lives, including my own." She smiled at that and continued on with the conversation. She told how this boy's parents had given up on him some time ago and gave the child to her and her husband to raise. She said, "We've done our best, but he is way more than we can handle, and we don't dare to leave him alone in the house for fear of what he will steal or destroy." She told me that she heard we don't take anyone under 18 without their parents, so she couldn't bring him before now. "He just turned 18, so here he is, and he's all yours. All I have to say is two things: #1 you'd better be 'The Miracle Man,' and #2 he knows not to call us to come and get him. He's all yours." She turned and left a scared young man in my office on Christmas Eve. The real "Miracle Worker" began to do His thing and this young man changed his ways, got a job, and later acquired an apartment. He grew up with the help of Jesus and a group of people who loved and set standards for him. He made it and never had to return to the shelter. He got a better Christmas gift then he could have imagined.

CHAPTER 27

In the midst of the joy, there are moments where the emotions that come out are hard to express. I was at a conference, and I got a call from my wife that Joyce was in a coma in the hospital. She had a major brain hemorrhage and the outlook was grim. I headed for home, but while in transit I received the call I feared. The family had the doctors unhook her from life support and she went home to be with Jesus. Now for her, that's not a bad thing, but it sure left a huge hole in all of our hearts. Joyce had been with us when it was only her, my wife, and myself praying every morning for the Holy Spirit to lead and care for this ministry. She made things for the residents as she knit and sewed many pairs of mittens and scarves she made out of love for them. I wish she was here to see all Jesus has accomplished, and all the churches that are sharing their hearts and finances with us. Some in the shelter created a monument in her honor in the park where we now have the baptismal. Special people like Joyce come once in a lifetime. She, like Spike, is now truly sheltered by Jesus.

One day a young pregnant lady showed up at the shelter. She was 8 ½ months along and no one would take her in. All the shelters were full and no family members had any room for her. My heart cried out when I heard her story. Blessings, however, were on the way for her and the shelter. The ladies all scrambled to host a baby shower for her, and people were moved in their hearts to care for this young girl. She received some great gifts and all the items she received were things she didn't already have because she only had the clothes on her back. It's tough enough to be a man on the streets, but I can't imagine the fear of this young girl who could have literally given birth to her child on the streets. Thankfully, she didn't, and this beautiful, newborn baby girl was born and moved into the shelter in the arms of her young mommy. What we all saw was amazing. The men in the shelter all became like a bunch of daddies. That little girl was hardly put down at all. One after another carried her around and made fools of themselves as they spoke in "fluent baby talk." To hear them speak was hilarious! Many were separated from their own families, so this baby was like medicine for their souls. I would love to hear the stories being told to that little girl as she grows up. She didn't have one daddy; she had a shelter full of them. My wife reminded me of one man in particular that blessed her heart while he held the baby in his arms. He would sing "Jesus Loves Me," and that tiny little face stared at him as though she knew every word. Now her mommy had fears, I am sure, but that baby only felt the love of a bunch of men that many people didn't want around. These men made her feel loved and special. Too bad adults couldn't see those men through that baby's eyes.

One of the questions I get asked many times as I travel and speak is, "Don't you feel afraid to have your wife living right next to those kind of people?" If they could see how gentle these men can be and the love they have for me and my wife they would never ask that question. Actually, what I tell them is that I would not want to see what would happen to anyone who attempted to hurt my wife. Some people have pit bulls, she has her guys. They would never make it off the property. One day someone came to the front door of the house. The men only saw a large person whom they did not recognize and the person was dressed pretty rough. They were not long getting to the house to check on my wife because I was away. There was no threat, but it showed both of us that when I travel and she does not, she would be well protected. How many people can say they have 60 bodyguards? She surely can!

CHAPTER 28

A NEAT THING happened as we were now taking in families. I needed ladies to serve on staff. Tinker and his wife Amy had been separated all this time because we couldn't take in women. She had been a nanny for her grandchildren. They were now school age, so Amy could leave and the family was just fine. I approached Tinker one day and asked, "Do you think Amy would like to join you as part of my staff?" He beamed all over and said, "I'll ask her!" She jumped at the opportunity to live together with her husband once again. All I could offer them was a room in the church. You would have thought I offered them the Trump Plaza. They were so excited. Together, they make an awesome team to care for the families. Just recently, I was in need of a cook. I didn't realize it, but Amy used to be a cook at a restaurant that offers homemade meals. Of course she was! The meals are awesome, and I can tell you, Pastor Berry is blessed by them as well! I may not be homeless, but I sure do enjoy good cooking. Just another blessing from God for taking in "those kind of people."

The church has been full of families now for a while. I realize that I will probably not be allowed to continue on forever as we are presently operating. The church is not up to code for a homeless shelter, as has been explained to me very clearly in the past. So, as I find mattresses in my office in the morning, I realize we are at the point where something must change. Therefore, I go back to "Dad" and tell Him my situation. It's not that I do not grasp the truth that He is fully aware of it already, but I needed to know what to do to move forward. A couple of days later, one of my neighbors told me that the huge house and barn on the corner lot that is connected to the church property was for sale. I explained I saw the sign, but I had no money. He went on to explain how badly a bank wanted to move it. They had repossessed it from the owners and simply desired to get it off their books. He said, "They are asking $39,500 for it." I replied, "You mean $139,500, right?" He said, "No. They want it off the books, so check with the realtors and get the information." I did, and they told me it was true. They asked if I would like to examine the property and I said, "Sure. Why not?" Doesn't cost a penny to look. It was an old farm house and barn that was built in 1930. Both the house and barn were in excellent condition. The house had been redone and was in amazing shape. The realtor explained that by the following Monday (it was already Thursday), the bank was going to decide to whom it would sell the property. Others were interested and made cash offers above the asking price. She asked if I wanted to make a bid on the place. I did, but there were a few problems facing me. #1 I had no money, and #2 I had not asked the church for authority to purchase the home by taking out a loan if necessary. So I had no authority to do anything besides pray. So without authority and no money, I said "Yes, I do." I would like to bid $50,000 with the provision that I can get a loan to pay for it. I will need at least 30 days before closing on the deal. She said she would put in my bid.

In the meantime, a Jesus thing was already taking place. Dr. Gary Hoag, who goes by the title of "Generosity Monk," was scheduled to speak at our weekend services. Gary is an international speaker who spoke at the National Conference in San Diego, the same time that I did. He heard my story and had been using it as an illustration as he traveled and spoke. He's a man of incredible faith! I told him about the possibility of obtaining this place to be used as a family shelter. He said, "Let's walk around the building and pray, asking Jesus to make it happen." We did, and then Dr. Hoag shared all weekend about how God moves to meet needs for those who trust Him. What a weekend for a seminar on God supplying in miraculous ways. He added, "You folks are experiencing this very thing with the shelter." He showed how it is never money you seek, but the power of God in prayer. God is our instrument of success, and not money. I thought, "Oh, Jesus. I see you painted a picture for me so clearly. I know the house is ours!" I was so excited to see how Jesus was going to get this house. But He had some tests coming, again, before we would get it.

I almost forgot to share a sub story to the whole ordeal. Prior to the family losing their home, the man would have a drink and then call me periodically to curse me, because he didn't like living next to homeless people. Now, God has such a sense of humor! Instead of him getting rid of us, God gets rid of him. He no longer is burdened with having to live next to a homeless shelter. I love Jesus!

Well, Monday morning came and I got a call from the realtor. She informed me my bid was refused, not because it wasn't high enough but because they wanted a cash bid, no loans, period. She asked me if I wanted to make a cash bid right now that she can forward to the bank before a decision is made. Now remember, I have no money and no authority from the church to make a bid. But we are having a quarterly business meeting in less than two weeks and I am counting on them saying yes. You know how churches normally operate, though. You call a business meeting and set up a committee to gather information and return with a recommendation back to the church. There was no time for that now, so I made a decision after praying and discussing this with Dr. Hoag to go for it. I made a bid of $50,000 cash for the building. That bid was accepted, so now I believed I had at least four weeks to get the church's approval and raise the money or get a loan. Boy, was I wrong. Jesus was not going to make it that easy. Oh, no! On Thursday of that week, I got a call from the realtor informing me that the Bank of California now wanted a fax sent to them by noon on Friday showing that I had the $50,000 cash in the bank. I assured her that was no problem.

There are times when I realize just how dumb a man God chose for all this, because no man with an ounce of intelligence would ever put himself in such a crazy position. He would know better. Each time I felt like there was no way this ministry could possibly continue, Jesus did a miracle and then I would feel foolish for not believing. So I said, "You're not going to get me this time. I have learned my lesson!" I relate myself many times to the Apostle Peter, quick to shove my foot into my mouth and with a size 13 shoe that is not very comfortable. The case that I believe relates to my situation is when Peter wanted to try walking on water. Most have heard the story even if they are not all that familiar with the Bible. It is found in Matthew 14. Jesus comes out to His disciples, who are in a boat on the lake. They are in a boat and He is simply walking on water! I would have loved to have seen that! Peter must have thought it was pretty cool, because he asks Jesus to tell him to come to him, all the time believing he could walk on water also at Jesus' command. Jesus tells him to come on and he does! He starts walking on water, because he's not smart enough to know he can't. What happens? All of a sudden, he gets smart enough to know he can't walk on water, so he sinks like a rock and cries out for Jesus to save him. The sad part is he was doing it until he examined all the practical reasons that pointed to the fact it could not be done. I can only imagine the look of disappointment on the face of Jesus. Peter learned a lesson that day, and it was that sometimes you must disregard what makes perfect human sense and if Jesus says, "Do it," just do it. But, Peter later learned from that mistake.

In the Gospel of John, chapter 21, Peter is asked to believe what his common sense told him not to believe once again. He and the other fishermen had been out all night and caught nothing. Jesus appeared in the morning and inquired as to how much luck they have had at catching the fish. Peter shouted back, “We haven’t caught a thing all night.” What happened next must have caught Peter by surprise. Jesus told them to cast the net over the right side of the boat and they would find some fish. Now think about that for just one moment. Trained and highly-skilled fishermen have fished this area all night long. There is no way that they have failed to throw that net over the boat from bow to stern and side to side. No way! Now Jesus calmly stated if you throw over the right side of the boat you will catch fish? Why should Peter, the same man who walked on water until he knew better, simply blindly obey this time? He had not forgotten the miracle he was a part of, and on top of that, Jesus is now resurrected from the grave. I believe with all my heart that Peter was thinking, “Jesus, you aren’t getting me this time! I will believe the unbelievable, as I have seen it before.” So he threw the net over the right side of the ship, and lo and behold, he caught fish where he knew there were no fish to be caught. Why? Jesus told him!

I feel that is exactly where I was at the moment I was asked to have a bank send a fax stating I had $50,000 cash and I did not have a penny. So, what do you do in a case like that? Yup, I called a bank in town and not even one with which we currently had an account. I asked to speak to a commercial loan officer. The man came to the phone and

I began to explain my situation. I said that I needed to purchase the house next to the shelter to make into a family shelter. I shared how I had no money and no authority from the church to ask for a loan of any kind, but needed his bank to tell a bank in California that I had $50,000 cash in his bank. You probably won't believe it, but that man laughed at me. He thought it was a prank. I quickly assured him I was very serious, and he laughed even harder! As I travel and share this story, I get the same response from those listening. They laugh, too! When he stopped laughing and actually grasped that I was serious, he explained that this would be totally against bank policy. He told me it would take at least 30 days to get someone to see the property, and even if it was a steal, that would not change anything. So I asked if he had a boss, and he informed me that he did. I asked if I could speak to him. A man came on the phone and I said, "I am Pastor Berry." He said he knew who I was and what I was doing with the homeless shelter. He then asked what it was I wanted. I told him the same thing I told the other gentleman. Guess what? He laughed, too! But the difference was when he stopped laughing, he asked me to come to his office at 9:00am the next day and tell him the entire story. The next morning, I decided to throw the net over the right side of the boat, knowing full well that there were no fish, simply because I believed this is what Jesus was telling me to do. There was no way He was making me feel foolish for not believing He would do it this time.

I arrived at the bank and was greeted by this gentleman and was invited into his office. We sat down and he said, "Tell me the whole story. Why do you want to do this?" I shared how Jesus reminded me of what it was like to lose everything, but have both my parents. He seemed genuinely moved by the story. In fact, I knew he was by what took place next. He reached into his desktop and picked up his business card. He handed it to me and said, "Take this to the realtor and have her call me with whatever information that bank deems necessary. I will then send a fax before noon today stating you have $50,000 cash in my bank without you signing a thing." He quickly added, "I've heard some of the stories about you building a shelter and operating it all the while having no idea where the monies will come from. I believe you will raise the funds in time, but if not just come and see me and I will have your back." I caught a whole boatload of fish in my net while fishing in an empty hole. Jesus followed up Dr. Hoag's lessons from Scripture with one done before our very eyes that day. Jesus continues to show me He is the "Great I am" and not the "Great I Was." Praise God that was accomplished. My bid is safe and now I can concentrate on the next two important things, getting the approval from the church, and raising $50,000 in the next month. A piece of cake for Jesus. I know from a human standpoint it sounds kind of overwhelming, but I have now learned to "walk on water," so this is no big deal.

There is already a quarterly business meeting scheduled, so we do not have to go through the process of having a special business meeting to present this to the church. What's great is I have full confidence in the members currently attending the church. They have become a truly united group after all we've been through the past few years. They have learned to look at Jesus and not the checkbook when a situation arises in which we are confident that Jesus is leading us in a particular direction. I have come to love and appreciate those who have chosen to be members of a church that fails to offer all the 'bells and whistles" that most churches enjoy. When the subject was brought up to move forward, trusting Jesus to pull off a miracle, there was a 100% vote to go for it. I just love this stuff! Now, in the meantime, the bank contacted the realtor to ask if we would allow them to have a couple of extra weeks before closing as there were some paperwork messes due to it being a repossessed house. I said we would definitely grant their request. Wasn't that nice of me? Yeah, right! I was jumping up and down, praising Jesus for giving me more time to hit the road to share the need and raise the funds. I knew we couldn't afford any payments, so I needed to raise the entire amount, and two extra weeks was like getting manna dropped down from heaven.

Jesus used these next weeks to show me His love poured out through His people, and in some extraordinary ways. It began with Ronnie's two sons breaking their piggy banks and giving all they had saved so the children would have a home. Dr. Hoag called to say, "I sold one of my favorite fishing rods so I would have a part in this and my wife sold some of her special baskets and dishes so she could have a part in this also." Now I admit it would take a lot of these small amounts to reach $50,000 but I could see Jesus' signature all over it. As I traveled and spoke, God moved hearts so monies began coming in from all over. Once again, Pastor Bill Cripe asked me to speak at Faith Evangelical Free Church in Waterville, Maine. They had given $30,000 to the other project and provided quarterly giving after that. When I spoke at this church, it was getting near the end of my period of time for the closing. What happened the day I spoke blew my socks off. When I finished, people were literally throwing money at me; Lines were forming so they could share a word of encouragement and give me money. At the end of the day, they had their scheduled business meeting and what was given individually and agreed upon at the meeting came to $32,000. With what I already had raised, we now had $50,000. So I could write a check for the house, paying cash! But, that wasn't what Jesus used to move me the most.

As I walked into the foyer to greet folks as they left the service, I had something happen that moved me to tears. A little boy was approaching me with his head down and feet shuffling. His mom and dad were behind him telling him it was okay to go to me. His arm was outstretched and his fist clasped holding something in his little hand. As he approached me, his mom said, "Pastor Berry, would you put your hand out please?" I did as he asked, and then he asked me to open my hand as he had something for me. He then opened his hand and a few coins landed in my hand. I do not remember the exact amount. Then this tiny little child with eyes still looking at his feet said, "This is for the little children." As a result, I left that day with $32,000 and a few cents. That few cents will touch my heart for the rest of my life. I knew then, without a shadow of a doubt, that Jesus was moving us to build this home and it would affect more than the residents. It would be a way to change the heart of a nation, starting with a new generation, one of whom just gave what little he had because Jesus touched his heart.

We now own the buildings with no mortgages, and our hearts are excited about what the future holds for the homeless. The engineer who drew up the plans for a new shelter came to me with some unexpected news. He said because of the angles in the house and barn, it would be cheaper to tear down the barn and put a shelter in its place. The house could only be a family residence and not used as a commercial shelter. So we are making plans to tear down the barn and put up a 48-bed family shelter, and a fenced-in area for the little children. It looks like the house will end up being used as a medical facility and offices for our social workers, which means we will be able to have them all on site. God's plans did not fully line up with mine, but it is all going to come together in the end. Once again, we will begin a project with no money, only Jesus, and I have learned that He is way more than enough to get the job done. I pray this book, which I truly believe is something that the Holy Spirit guided me to write (especially since I am not a writer by any stretch of the imagination) will draw believers from all over to come and see the miracles of God at work on a daily basis. And I am already praying He will move hearts like those little children, to desire to share in this project.

CHAPTER 29

NOW IN THE midst of all of this, my wife came to me with a question. "What happens to me if Jesus takes you home first? Since we live in a parsonage, owned by the church, where would I live?" Great question. Because all of my energies and time are spent on the homeless, I did not give any thought to our own future. I replied, "We will begin to look for homes this week." The problem is that we do not have much money. I then went on to say, "Let's pray and see what Dad will do for us." We set a dollar amount for a home for which we would have enough for a down payment. It had to be in the range of $30,000-$40,000. Now if you know anything about the cost of houses, that amount of money might be enough to buy a shed in the middle of nowhere. But we had two things in our favor, three if you count Jesus. My mom wanted to help, and I had a fantastic contractor on my staff named Brett Cullen. He was so good he had taken a crew in the past to work at President Bush's mansion in Kennebunk, Maine. Of course he just happened to be on staff at this time. He volunteered to help us find a home that would fit our budget, and would willingly put a crew together to make it work. My wife fell in love with this 1910 home that looked like the house in the comedy show *The Munsters*. It would have made a great home for Halloween! As my wife and I, along with Brett, were going through the house, I was praying that Brett would say this could not work. I mean, it was really ugly! But Brett sided with my wife and kept saying, "This old house was well built. It has a great foundation and the rooms are all square. I can fix this up to be a great home." We put in a low bid, but because it had been for sale for seven years and no offers, they jumped at it. Because of all the needs for repairs, we had to come up with enough money for an extra down payment to the bank to cover all quotes of costs on top of the selling price. It looked like it wasn't going to happen, as we didn't have all of the money to put down. My mom, however, wanted us to have it, so she made up the difference. Here I am at 65 years of age and Jesus didn't think I was humble enough, I guess. He had me swallow my pride and let my mom help me. That was tough, but I thank God for a loving mom.

Now it was time to get the house ready to live in, and that meant a total overhaul of the house from the cellar to the top of the chimney. What Jesus showed me next will be a story I share the rest of my life. Brett asked for volunteers to work on the Pastor's new home. Hands went up all over the place. For the next seven months, Brett took a crew that kept changing as residents came and went, with various levels of skills, and they labored six days a week. In the end, they transformed a house into a home, like Jesus transformed their lives at the shelter. No one would believe what this place looked like the day we first looked at it—No more than anyone would believe the condition many lives were in before they were transformed by Jesus. You may not call it a miracle, but you will never convince me or my wife that it was anything but a miracle. And now we are in our own home, and we are also sheltered by Jesus.

Now, what's next for this crazy ministry that Jesus has risen up? Well, I believe Jesus has given me a vision of the future for when the 48-bed shelter is up and running. Not like the Apostle John on Patmos, or anything like that, but it is what's been put on my heart and mind. I am expecting Jesus to raise up a business that has all homeless people as workers, to develop a product that can be labeled "made by the homeless" and marketed internationally. This will help those who are young to develop a marketable skill that can translate into a future job opportunity with other companies. Right now, felons are not being hired by some companies. My goal is to invite owners and CEO's of companies to come and observe these people at work and to show them their new work history and prove they can be good employees for their companies. I would have an account set up where their wages, all but a small stipend, are set aside until they are ready to leave. They would then receive a check for their wages that would allow them to have enough for a down payment on an apartment or home, and a vehicle. They would leave with the opportunity to remain off of the streets. Imagine the glory that would go to Jesus with this in our country today!

And from there? Well, the story continues…

ABOUT TRINITY HOMELESS SHELTER

Trinity Homeless Shelter is completely staffed by the homeless. WHAT? You read correctly! Many of the folks who have walked in through the doors of this shelter with nothing, are actually running the place! Many have lost jobs and homes, but have found a new lease on life by entering into the shelter, finding purpose and wholeness and giving themselves to the mission and vision of the organization.

This shelter, located in Skowhegan, Maine, could be a template for other churches to follow. The somewhat unorthodox method of having the residents run the facility, feeding, clothing and helping others find gainful employment is nothing short of miraculous...and it works! The staff (residents) gets room and board for their positions. They work in the office, the food pantry, the laundry, kitchen, firing up the wood boiler, and various other chores—all requirements for an on-going operation, so that when the next needy soul shows up at the door, there is shelter from the storm.

If you are interested in learning more, or if you would like to contribute to this unique ministry that has served so many, please visit shelterbyjesus.org or write to us at the address below:

Trinity Homeless Shelter
12 McClellan St Ste 2
Skowhegan, Maine 04976

Thank you for your interest in the shelter. I pray that you have been inspired to consider serving wherever God has placed you.

— *Pastor Richard Berry*

ABOUT THE AUTHOR

The Rev. Richard Berry is the Senior Pastor of Trinity Evangelical Free Church and the Skowhegan Miracle Homeless Shelter in Skowhegan, ME. Richard has over 30 years in ministry and holds ordinations with the EFCA and the ABC.

In 2007, Richard was approached by a longtime acquaintance who would be homeless in just a few short days. Richard provided a couch in a church Sunday school room, and the influx of those in need of shelter began crossing the threshold of TEFC. Through the process of housing the homeless in the church, Richard saw 80% of his congregation leave, including immediate family members because they couldn't worship "with those kinds of people." Facing closure from state officials, a dwindling congregation and dwindling finances, Richard simply dropped to his knees and prayed.

Today, through faith and the power of the Living God, almost 1,000 men have been provided shelter, food, and spiritual nourishment in the small rural landscape of central Maine through the ministry of Richard and TEFC. The operation is run solely on in-kind donations and the hand of God. The shelter, with a volunteer staff of homeless men, continues to provide shelter to all in need.

The new shelter, with a grand opening in January 2012, boasts a commercial kitchen, commercial laundromat, and a handicap room with oxygen hookup. In addition, the men housed in the ministry have direct access to a free medical clinic each Friday, social and behavioral health services, addiction counseling services, employment services, and an opportunity to gain a seminary level education through the EFCA's Gateway Theological Institute.

The Rev. Richard Berry and the ministry at TEFC has been detailed in several publications including: *Downeast Magazine*, *The Christian Science Monitor*, *The EFCA Today*, several local newspapers and media outlets, as well as local news segments. Furthermore, Richard has been listed in "Who's Who in America" and was honored with the 2010 Crisis and Counseling Agency of the Year award by the State of Maine.

Pastor Berry is available for speaking at your church or group.

Contact him at: *trinity_efree@yahoo.com*